God Outside the Box
A Story of Breaking Free

PATRICIA PANAHI

authorHOUSE

AuthorHouse™
1663 Liberty Drive, Suite 200
Bloomington, IN 47403
www.authorhouse.com
Phone: 1-800-839-8640

Some names have been changed to protect the privacy of the individual.

© 2008 Patricia Panahi. All rights reserved.

No part of this book may be reproduced, stored in a retrieval system, or transmitted by any means without the written permission of the author.

First published by AuthorHouse   4/14/2008

ISBN: 978-1-4343-6776-1 (e)
ISBN: 978-1-4343-6775-4 (sc)

Printed in the United States of America
Bloomington, Indiana

This book is printed on acid-free paper.

The words spirit, soul, and Higher Self refer to different aspects of our spiritual nature. For the sake of simplicity, they are used interchangeably to refer to the spiritual part of us.

To Mark Johnson,
a.k.a. *Chris* in this book.

AND

In memory of Ed.

Acknowledgements

First and foremost, I would like to acknowledge my husband, Mark Coates, for always believing in me. I'd also like to thank members of my writing group, Marianna, Frances, and Brendan for listening to the many drafts of this book. Many thanks to Cristina Salat and Dr. Mark Panek for their review and insights, Sarah Blanchard for her editorial assistance, and Dr. Louise Wisechild for helping me with the prologue. I also want to express my appreciation for the assistance and suggestions of author Karen Joy Fowler and all the workshop participants at the Maui Writers Retreat. Last, but not least, I would like to acknowledge all the individuals, teachers, and authors who have directly and indirectly guided me over the years on my journey of self-discovery.

Prologue

I wish I could show you when you are lonely or in darkness the astonishing light of your own being.

- Hafiz

When I was eight, I lost my most precious possession, a rubber ball I had purchased with the first dollar I ever earned. It was the size of a volleyball, pink and smooth and soft. I liked to bounce it on the sidewalk and show it to everyone I met. I'd tell them the story of how I'd helped my mom with housework and she'd given me a whole dollar and I'd used it to buy my very own ball.

A few weeks later, I was visiting Nana in New Jersey and we went to a military picnic and clam bake. Women in bright dresses and hats served potato salad and buttered corn on the cob at picnic tables. A brawny man with a crew cut pulled clams out of a huge, steaming vat and opened the shells with a knife. Nana showed me how to season them with lemon and dip them in butter and pop them in my mouth. I liked the rubbery, ocean taste of the clams and went back for a second helping.

I met other kids by the lake and we played dodge ball with my pink ball late into the afternoon. Then, without warning, the sky darkened and a storm rolled in with gusty winds and rain. We had to pack up and leave quickly, but I couldn't find my prized ball. I cried out in anguish while the adults grabbed my arm and shoved me into the car. This was my first experience of how the winds could rise and carry away something precious to me.

Back at Nana's house, I just couldn't believe that I had lost my most prized possession. "I'll buy you another one," Nana had said, but it would never be the same. That pink rubber ball meant more to me than a mere child's toy. It represented independence and self-reliance—the belief that I could make my own way.

With knots in my stomach and tears rolling down my cheeks, I bolted up to the bedroom and opened the drawer with my grandmother's Bible, a book I knew she regarded as holy. At that young age, I wasn't quite sure what religion I was supposed to follow. My mom had been raised a Catholic and my dad had been Moslem, but neither practiced nor taught me anything about the religious beliefs of their families. Nevertheless, a part of me had always felt that a spiritual being I could neither see nor touch nor hear had created me and protected me.

I ran my fingers across the worn, brown leather Bible cover and asked for a sign. Flipping it open, I pointed to a line on the page and read: *In the Lord, put your trust.* (Psalms 11:1) Upon reading these words, a loving feeling washed over me, like I was being embraced by angel arms and reassured that everything would turn out okay. Breathing a sigh of relief, I sprinted down the stairs to find my grandmother. I informed her that my ball would be found, that the Bible said so. Within the hour, a friend called and said her teenage daughter had found the ball and she would bring it to the house. On that day, I learned to ask for help and to trust that it would be provided, but how or what or by whom was still a mystery.

In my youth and early twenties, I explored numerous religions, but nothing ever really stuck. I always wanted to know what other groups thought or practiced or believed. I couldn't accept the idea that one group had the whole truth and everyone else was wrong, or confused, or infidels, or a cult, or going to burn in hell for all time. I wasn't content with one book or one set of beliefs or practices. To limit my thinking for religious purposes was like living in a cubicle and not being allowed to look over the wall and see what was going on outside. I wanted to think for myself, to study, to analyze and to practice without inhibitions. Why would God only accept the practices and prayers of one particular group and not others? An omniscient God couldn't be that petty, could he—or she?

I finally concluded that I just didn't know and floundered in a spiritual void for a time. But when I was diagnosed with a serious illness and reunited with a childhood friend, I cracked and fell to pieces. Deep, buried emotions erupted to the surface, shaking me to my core. Propelled to seek answers and find inner peace, I tumbled into a spiritual adventure that exploded my concepts of reality and opened me to a brave new world where souls talk, trees emit energy fields, rocks have life, and God is everywhere.

Chapter One: Beginnings

I go into the Moslem mosque, the Jewish synagogue, and the Christian church and I see one altar.

– Rumi

Catholicism

When I was five years old, Nana dolled me up in a Sunday dress and bonnet, all pink and lace with shiny black shoes, and took me to Saint Mary of the Falls for Catholic mass.

The year was 1956. We were living in Olmsted Falls, Ohio back then, Mommy and Daddy and my little sister and me, in a studio apartment attached to my grandparents' place. Nana and Papa and mommy's brother Ed lived in the main house, a one-story with a brick façade on Columbia Avenue. Ed was ten and tall with dark hair and thick glasses. I idolized Ed. He was my best friend.

We reached the church. Nana arranged her hat and veil and smoothed out her skirt. At the entrance, she dipped the fingers of one hand in a cup of water and touched her forehead, left shoulder, right shoulder, and chest, then grasped my hand and we stepped inside. I thought about how Mommy never took me to church. Papa says she's just not the church-going type. I guess Papa wasn't either.

Inside the church, we stopped at a table with lots and lots of candles. "We'll light a candle for you." My grandmother picked up a taper.

"Why, Nana?" I looked up at her with big blue eyes.

"So that God will bless you," she replied, guiding my hand and helping me light the candle myself.

I didn't know what that meant, but it sounded good. I stood up straight, taking pride in my little candle flame, its light blending in with the others like a bright star.

Nana led me down the aisle and I craned my neck to view the cathedral's ceilings; they looked as high as the sky.

Other people were all dressed up like me, nice and pretty. We slid into a bench and I sat quietly while Nana chatted with strangers. I was bored soon enough and got up on my knees to look around. A few boys in gowns fussed around the altar. Above them, a statue of a man with long hair hung on a cross. Blood oozed out of his hands and feet. He looked scary.

"Who's that, Nana?" I yanked my grandmother's arm and pointed to the cross.

Nana followed my finger and smiled. "That's Jesus. He was God's son. He died for our sins."

I scrunched my face. "What's a sin, Nana?"

"Bad things that people do, sweetheart." She patted my head.

Mommy says I'm bad sometimes. Does that mean I've sinned? I gulped and looked up at Jesus again.

Organ music filled the vast hall and the chatter faded away.

A man in a long black robe stepped onto the stage. Everybody picked up their books and began to sing. The people behind us sounded like a scratched record. I cupped my hands over my ears. We sat down for a while then everyone kneeled and prayed with their beads. Nana pressed a string of blue beads into the palm of my hand. I stretched it out; the blue beads sparkled like gems. I wanted to put them around my neck because they looked so pretty, but I watched my grandmother and tried to mimic her prayer movements instead. I wondered what all this meant.

After the prayers, the people stood up and sang again. It was awfully loud. When the other children were herded out to Sunday school by a scowling nun, I clung to Nana's arm. She motioned to the nun to let me stay with her.

The priest began his sermon. He talked really loud and moved his hands a lot. I didn't understand most of it, but I learned that there was some terrible place called hell where all the bad people went. I remembered being bad when I was four. Papa had two Great Danes back then. Whenever I wanted to play in the backyard, they jumped all over me, licking and slobbering and knocking me down. They were big and scary and I didn't like them and I wanted to go outside and play so finally I snuck out and left the gate open and they ran away. No one could find them. I never admitted my guilt, but somehow they all knew it was me—adults know these things. Nana had been really mad at me. She said I'd done a bad thing. Was I going to hell?

Wrapping my arms around myself, I slid closer to Nana, comforted by the warmth and touch of her body. A pot-bellied man sitting in the next pew began to snore. I let out a soft giggle, but quickly repressed it when Nana gave me a firm nudge. Leaning back in the seat, I gazed up at the glass windows etched with haloed saints. The morning had been cloudy, but now a beam of light broke through and shone through the window. One of the saints looked like an angel stretching her wings. I smiled and waved.

The clouds cleared and the sun came out and the figures in the glass windows lit up and came to life. I watched them in awe and wonder.

After the service, Nana shoved me in front of Father Joseph. "This was her first mass," she said proudly. I looked up at the priest in his long, black robe and tried to hide behind my grandmother. Father Joseph asked if I enjoyed my first day at church.

I peeked up from behind Nana's purse and said, "I liked the angels."

Islam

My friends say that Daddy talks funny, but I think that's just the way Daddy talks. When he can't remember an English word he snaps his fingers over and over and says *wha-cha-ma-call-it*. Daddy's from a place called Iran. It's on the other side of the world. Nana says that he used to be a graduate student at Columbia University, but after he married Mommy, his family in Iran stopped sending him money, so he had to go to work with Papa, Mommy's father, in the ink factory.

My parents met at the Natural History Museum in New York while Mommy was on a high school field trip. Nana says she and Mommy used to burst out laughing because Daddy used funny words to explain things. Nana says I look like Mommy, the same big blue eyes and fair hair. I like looking like Mommy—I think she's pretty. My sister has Daddy's exotic look with dark hair and brown eyes.

When I was six, we moved to our own house, a small three-bedroom with a fenced-in yard in Elyria, Ohio. Life was ordinary, predictable, and secure. I wore saddle shoes, wiggled my hips in a vain attempt to keep my hula hoop in the air, watched Howdy Doody and Captain Kangaroo, and loved trick-or-treating on Halloween. I attended Eaton Elementary, a spare sock full of marbles in tow, in hope of winning bigger and prettier ones. During Ed's visits, we'd explore the local woods, share our favorite comic books, see scary movies like the *Blob*, or stroll up to the local Dairy Queen for chocolate-covered ice cream on a stick. My summers were spent exploring the neighborhood and nearby forest and stream, usually staying out until dusk. "Just be home for supper," Mommy would say.

But when I was nine, my world flipped upside down.

Daddy went back to Iran to take care of family business, but then discovered that he couldn't return to America because he hadn't served in the Iranian military. Unable to come home, undoubtedly missing his wife and kids, he said we should all move to Iran, that we would have a better life there. He could work as an architect because he'd graduated from Tehran University before he came to the States. We would have a nice house, he said, and we could even have servants to help with the chores.

I didn't know anything about Iran, couldn't begin to understand what this meant. All I knew was that Daddy had been gone for over a year. I missed Daddy.

Mommy reluctantly agreed. Yes, we would move to Iran.

I remember the day everything fell apart. My sister and I were at Nana's house because Nana was taking care of us while Mommy was busy handling all the details for our move to Iran.

The phone rang, and suddenly Nana's voice got high and hysterical. I crept up the few steps to the dining room where Nana was talking on the phone. She hung up and turned to me, her eyes red, her face contorted. "Your mother is gone," she said. "She's run off with another man. She's not going to Iran."

I just stood there, staring at my grandmother, watching her attempt to be strong, to pull herself together, to hold back the tears. Turning away, I shuffled into the living room, plopped onto the couch, and flipped through a *Superman* comic book while my sister's wails shook the house.

* * * * *

Living in Iran is downright weird. I can't wear shorts. Can't talk to boys. Can't go out unescorted. Everyday we eat rice and strange-tasting lamb stews. The writing looks like squiggly worms about to wiggle their way off the page. I don't know the language, so they push me back to first grade—I should've been in the fourth. Walls are everywhere, high walls made of brick and stone and mortar; they surround the yards, the schools, the government buildings, even the empty lots. Daddy says they're there to keep us safe, but they remind me of a prison I once saw on TV.

And I have no mother.

People keep saying things that they don't mean, like the custom called *ta'arof*. When you're a guest in someone's house and they offer you food or drink, you have to say no, even though you may be starving or dying of thirst. The hostess will insist, and you have to refuse at least three times before accepting. Anything less is considered rude.

Before stepping onto the carpet, you have to take off your shoes, and every morning and once again when you come home from school, you have to greet everyone with salaam; otherwise, they get mad. Worst of all is the bathroom: a hole in the ground where you have to squat and do your business and wash yourself with a watering can, all the while praying that you won't fall in and be gobbled up and lost forever.

Everyone calls themselves Moslems, although I'm not exactly sure what that means, but being a Moslem is really important because if you want to insult someone, you call him a non-Moslem.

Daddy doesn't practice his religion. Doesn't believe that I should either. The family members, on the other hand, have their own opinions. They sit cross-legged on the scarlet Persian carpet, sipping Darjeeling tea from hour-shaped glasses with golden rims, a clump of sugar swelling their cheeks. The samovar bubbles on a squat table to one side of the room, a china tea pot with rose designs perched on top. "The daughter of a Moslem is Moslem," they say, speaking with their hands as much as their lips. "She must learn how to be one."

My mother is Catholic. Am I both?
But I have no mother.

The heated discussion continued in our house for several days. I wondered what a Moslem was. Daddy finally caved and, during the summer of my thirteenth birthday, I was sent to maktab, a religious school, to learn the ways of Islam.

The chador-clad maid hustled me through a labyrinth of narrow alleyways, past ancient mud and brick walls, garden groves bursting with bright red cherries and sour green plums, branches heavy with white mulberries reaching down to gently flowing streams, small shops displaying half carcasses of sheep, skinned and hanging in the window, fresh produce, rice, legumes, and dried fruit in open crates and barrels, and bakeries rich with the aroma of freshly-baked sangkak flat bread. She tugged my arm and pushed me along as I stared, open mouthed, at an old, dusty graveyard, its inhabitants long forgotten. "That's where they wash the dead," she said, pointing to a small brick and mud structure. I wanted to peek inside, but she dragged me away.

The maid finally stopped in front of a decrepit door etched in ancient designs. A small woman with a crinkled face and rotten teeth thrust her head through the opened door, hennaed hair spilling out from an oversized white scarf. She led us into a packed-dirt courtyard shaded by a sprawling walnut tree hanging over a pond. A rainbow-colored rooster strutted across our path. Chickens clucked and pecked. A goat tethered to a tree, grazed on a clump of weeds. To one side of the courtyard, boys and girls kneeled on straw mats, rocking back and forth, chanting their lessons. I was directed to join the others.

I smiled at a round-faced boy with mussed-up hair and asked his name.

Whack! My back stung. *Shabaji khanoum*, the teacher, whipped me with a wet reed that had been soaking in the pond.

"Pay attention, girl!" She thrust a small booklet in my face. We all opened to the first page. *Shabaji khanoum* began chanting the first part of the prayer, *"Allah o Akbar"* (God is great). We repeated in unison. *"Ashhad o Allah la elaha el ala"* (I give witness that there is one God), *"Ashad o Allah Mohamaden rasul ola,"* (I give witness that Mohammed is his prophet). "Learn this part for today," the teacher commanded. Leaning back on two cylinder-shaped pillows, she poured tea from a small glass into a saucer and sipped, one cheek bulging with a lump of sugar. The children rocked back and forth chanting the prayer. I joined in.

After the whack from the wet reed, I learned to give *Shabaji khanoum* my complete attention. She taught us that Mohammad was the last and final prophet of God and Islam the only complete religion. *Why don't all the Catholics know this?*

"These are the five basic duties of every Moslem," she said, leaning forward and glaring at each student. I shivered when her gaze landed on me.

"Write these down and memorize them for tomorrow."

"One: Give witness that there is only one God and that Mohammad is his prophet."

We bent over our notebooks and wrote furiously.

"Two: Pray five times a day. Three: Give alms to the poor."

I shook my hand to get rid of the cramping.

"Four: Fast during the month of Ramadan. Five: Make a pilgrimage to Mecca at least once in a lifetime."

Shabaji khanoum rose from her mat and hobbled amongst the students, making sure they had copied her teachings correctly. One boy got a smack in the head. He must have gotten the information wrong. The teacher made him copy all the rules down again from another boy's notebook.

I memorized the Arabic prayer and studied the meaning of the words in Farsi, the primary language spoken in Iran. I wondered why we had to pray in Arabic. *Isn't this prayer just for Arab people?*

"We must have complete obedience and submission to the will of God," said *Shabaji khanoum*, her crinkly face menacing. "Everything that happens in our lives is God's will."

I wondered why God would want to direct all the little events of my life. Didn't he have bigger and better things to do? Didn't I have any say in the matter, any choices of my own to make? Glancing up at *Shabaji khanoums's* scowling face; I felt it prudent to keep my conjectures to myself.

A month later, relieved to have completed the lesson so I wouldn't have to visit *Shabaji khanoum* again, I recited the prayer in proper Arabic to the accolades of family members. One relative fastened a gold chain and pendant around my neck. The pendant spelled *Allah*, the Arabic word for God. I remembered that Nana had given me a gold cross when I was six. I had felt protected wearing the cross, although I couldn't remember what had happened to it. Strangely, the *Allah* gave me the same feeling.

An older woman untied a white bundle and pulled out a *chador*, a large half circle of fabric with a pattern of tiny blue flowers. She draped it over my head and showed me how to cover my hair and fasten the *chador* under my neck so that my hands would be free to pray. The *chador* flowed down to my feet, covering every inch of me except my face. I turned to the mirror, startled to see a disembodied head like the man in the mirror in the Snow White fairy tale.

I'd noticed that some people wore the chador whenever they left the house, although no one in our family did. I had asked a *chadori* friend at school why she wore one. "My grandmother is religious," was her reply. "She gets upset if we leave the house bareheaded."

"But there must be other reasons people wear *chadors*."

"Of course," she said, pulling her *chador* half back over her head as we exited the walled-in school yard. Strands of her hair escaped the *chador* and blew in the breeze while the front *flapped* open to reveal her miniskirt, stocking-clad legs, and black leather pumps. In spite of the vice principal's efforts—she perpetually ripped the hems of uniforms so that they hung below the knees—the students were defiant, returning the next day in miniskirts, or mascara, or plucked eyebrows. A girl just had to be stylish when out in public.

"We cover ourselves because if men see our hair and the shapes of our bodies, they will get excited and can't control themselves," my friend replied, her lashes thick with black mascara.

I thought about this as we paced down the street. "So, you're saying that the women have to go to all this trouble to cover themselves up because the men are weak-willed? This makes no sense. If they get excited by seeing your hair, it's their problem, not yours. Why do you have to pay for it?"

My friend had no response.

The memory of my friend faded as I examined my new chador with its white background and pattern of tiny blue flowers, wondering why God didn't want to see my hair while I prayed.

My elderly relative lifted a bundle out of a chest and handed it to me reverently. Two embroidered blue velvet prayer mats enfolded a flat prayer stone from Mecca. I accepted my new gifts graciously..

Reveling in all the family attention, I began reciting my prayers. It was exciting at first, waking before dawn to a distant cock's crow, stealing into the bathroom in the dim morning light to perform the cleansing rituals, listening to the haunting chants of old Masht Ali, the help, as he chanted his prayers in a loud, sing-song manner— the only adult in the household who prayed.

But it didn't take long for the novelty to wear off. Getting up each day in the dawn chill was a bear—I was never much of a morning person. Trying to think of the meaning of the words, recite them correctly, and simultaneously perform the proper motions was demanding, taxing, especially at the crack of dawn. My prayers had become a chore, a rote recitation with no feeling, no lightness of the soul, no sense of connection. It was like my experience with Nana at the Catholic mass years ago, minus the angels.

I woke before dawn and groggily dragged myself out of bed. I had been performing my prayers for almost a month now. Shuffling into the bathroom for the cleansing ritual, I looked at my thirteen-year-old self in the bathroom mirror, blue eyes heavy with sleep. I didn't want to do this anymore. I didn't want to pray in a language I didn't understand or follow prescribed rituals that held no meaning for me. I knew this. Felt it in my bones. *Why pray in Arabic anyway? Doesn't God understand all languages?*

Slipping back into my bedroom, I folded my *chador*, placed it in the bottom of my dresser drawer, and crawled back into the delicious warmth of my bed.

ZOROASTRIANISM

I was twenty-one, teaching English at a private elementary school during the day and taking college classes at night. My sister was a full-time student at Tehran University, but making my own money was important to me, so I chose to work and study at the same time.

Scanning the list of paper assignments for my philosophy class, Zoroastrianism, the ancient religion of Iran, sounded intriguing. I'd heard that this had been the religion of the Persians prior to the Arab invasion, but when I asked my high school friends, they had dismissed it with a flick of their hands. "They're fire worshippers," they said. "They don't know any better."

Since Moslems tend to dismiss any religion other than their own, I wasn't convinced. While I would have preferred to find a Zoroastrian and ask questions, I didn't have the foggiest idea where to look for one, so I resigned to burying myself in the college library for hours on end.

I learned that this religion rose from the teachings of the prophet Zoroaster, also known as Zarathushtra. His writings go as far back as 1750 BCE, although the exact dates of his life are unknown. He taught his followers that there was only one God, whom he called *Ahura Mazda*, and that all evil came from another being called *Angra Mainyu*, later known as *Ahriman*--the devil. These beings, embodiments of good and evil, were engaged in a cosmic struggle. Humans could be allies in the struggle against evil by following the basic precepts of *Good Thoughts*, *Good Deeds*, and *Good Words*.

Zoroaster taught that when a person dies, he is judged by the actions of his life. If the good deeds outweigh the bad deeds, the soul enters paradise. If the opposite is true, the soul is cast into hell until the day of universal judgment. If the good and bad deeds are equal, the soul is consigned to limbo. Near the end of time, a savior will appear to resurrect the dead. All sinners, since they have already suffered in limbo or hell, will be purified by *Ahura Mazda* and other holy immortals or angels, and granted immortality. Evil will be defeated and *Ahriman* will be sealed in hell.

These ideas and beliefs seemed *very* familiar, and yet, Zoroaster's life predated the teachings of Mohammed, Jesus, and even Moses. *Interesting.*

The loudspeaker announced that the library was closing. Grabbing several books, I scurried to the counter to check them out. After lugging them all the way home on a crowded bus, I read through the night.

Zoroastrian temples always kept a fire burning. Fire, being a pure creation, became the symbol of *Ahura Mazda* much like the fish and cross that symbolized Christianity and the crescent that symbolized Islam. *So, they're not really fire worshippers after all. Hmmm.*

The *Avesta* is their holy book and Zoroastrian priests are called magi. *Were these the same magi who visited Jesus at his birth? Could they have been Zoroastrian priests?* More intrigued than ever, I dove into other historical accounts.

During the Achaemenid dynasty, 550 – 330 BCE, Zoroastrianism emerged as the dominant religion of the Persian Empire. By the time of the Sassanian dynasty, CE, 224 – 651, Zoroastrianism was practiced from the Middle East to the western border of China. It is believed by many historians to be the first monotheistic religion of the world.

During the 7th century CE, burning with religious zeal, Moslems from the Arab peninsula conquered Iran. Anyone who did not convert to Islam had to pay a special tax to Moslem authorities, a practice that continued until 1854.

Over the next six centuries, some Zoroastrians fled to China and India, while others gathered in central and eastern Iranian cities such as *Yazd* and *Kerman* where they paid their special taxes and were periodically persecuted. Many converted to Islam, but not all.

I imagined the Arab invasion—a swarm of sun-scorched men with dusty sandals, torn clothes, ox-hide shields, and swords sheathed in rags; nomads on swift camels, fired with religious zeal. I wondered how the proud Persians had felt, their empire conquered, their libraries burned, their priceless artifacts destroyed, their religion belittled. They bowed to the new religion of Islam, under the power of what they considered to be a horde of illiterate, desert-dwelling nomads. I imagined the fear of persecution, the desperation, the financial burden of taxes, the social stigma, the need to survive in a Moslem world where infidels or non-believers are second-class citizens, even to this day. How many paid lip service to Islam out of fear or necessity? And how many truly embraced this religion of the Arabs with their heart and souls?

The Persians are a passionate people; they love their exquisite gardens with bright flowers, shady trees, and the coolness of mosaic tiled fountains playing against the desert sun. They take great pleasure in large gatherings of family and friends, feasting on scrumptious dishes of rice and lamb prepared with great care. They savor their music, their dance, their poetry, and their wine. How did they reconcile the strict rules of Islam and its focus on the afterlife, with their own passion for life in the here and now?

While Zoroastrianism did not speak to me, nor draw me to learn more, I wondered what Iran would be like today if the Arabs had never invaded.

Hinduism

It was 1973. I was twenty-two and teaching at the Imperial Iranian Air Force Training Center in downtown Tehran. The Shah had decreed that all Air Force personnel learn English. The civilian English teachers were an eclectic cast of characters: Moslems, Jews, Bahai's, and Eastern Orthodox Armenian Christians. Most were Iranians educated in America or Great Britain. Added to this peculiar mix were a number of Pakistani Sunni Moslems and a few American rebels from the sixties who weren't sure what they were. While I had never seen these groups interact in the outside world, in this particular setting acceptance seemed to be the norm. I liked the diversity and made new friends.

One day during the mid-morning break, we gathered around a cinnamon-colored Formica table munching spicy *samosas*, made by the Pakistanis and sold in the cafeteria.

"They teach yoga classes at this place up near Tajrish," said one of the Americans, pushing long, unkempt hair back from his eyes. "Better yet, it's *free*."

"What is yoga?" asked an Iranian woman, prim and proper in her western suit, salon-styled hair, and overdone make-up.

"It's an ancient form of stretching exercise that strengthens the body and calms the mind."

Intrigued, a group of us decided to check it out. That same Friday, we piled into a car and headed up Old Shemiran Road. The house, located in an upscale neighborhood in northern Tehran, was owned by a prominent Iranian accountant who had secretly converted to Hinduism. Exquisite silk Persian carpets embellished marble floors. Two large French doors opened into a landscaped courtyard. Gossamer curtains billowed in the breeze. The place was open and light and inviting. The swami, a young American dressed in saffron robes, guided us through a series of yoga postures, most of which were too difficult for my inflexible body. My muscles screamed.

After the yoga lesson, another man dressed in white joined us and began playing a melon-shaped drum. The swami played the sitar and guided us in relaxation.

I lay flat on the carpet, focusing on each part of my body as directed. My muscles began to loosen and relax as a tingly sensation spread from my head to my toes. The exotic sounds of drum and sitar blended in a mystical harmony. I felt floaty, detached. My thoughts seemed less important, insignificant—I had trouble even holding on to them. My mind melded into a blissful harmony with the music. The notes danced around the room, and some part of me, released from physical limitations, joined the dance. I lost all sense of time and space.

When I opened my eyes, I was disoriented. I felt relaxed, heavy, as if I'd spent days in a Rip Van Winkle-type of slumber. The room seemed different somehow, the colors brighter, like I had been wearing dark glasses all my life and had just taken them off.

The swami talked about a religion called Hinduism, or at least one sect of it. He showed us copies of ancient texts called the *Upanishads* and claimed the original texts were written in Sanskrit over 5,000 years ago. "And this is a picture of God when he incarnated on earth as Krishna." We all stared at a blue man playing a flute surrounded by Indian girls. "Krishna taught man to love," the swami added.

A loving God. A smiling God. A God who danced and played. Such a new concept! I thought of Jesus hanging on the cross in the Catholic church, blood dripping from his hands and ankles; scenes from a movie about the Bible that portrayed an angry God chasing Adam and Eve out of the Garden of Eden and reducing Sodom and Gomorra to rubble; and the stern God of Islam who has no image, no form, yet who demands obedience and complete surrender to his will. I opened my eyes and examined the picture of Krishna again. His companions, the *Gopi* girls, wore smiles of total bliss.

The surrounding landscape was lush green, dotted with blooming flowers and animals, bursting with life, with love, with acceptance. Paradise.

Iran was certainly a Moslem country in 1973, people of the book, (Jews and Christians), and even Zoroastrians, were tolerated, though they were treated as second class citizens. Hinduism, however, was considered to be idol worship and was unacceptable. The prophet Mohamed had broken all idols and false images of God. So, the Hindu temple had to operate underground, in secret. Yet, like the forbidden fruit, it was alluring, tempting, possibly dangerous. I craved to know more.

Thirsting for a spiritual connection, a wholeness and inner peace, I began visiting the Hindu temple on Fridays, my day off from work. I kept these visits a secret from everyone except two of my colleagues, Bahman and his brother, who continued to visit the temple with me. I did not know what would happen to me if I were discovered, since even in modern Iran, changing your religion from Islam to *anything* else is against the law—but, I just *had to* find out, regardless of the consequences.

I practiced Hatha yoga and meditation, studied English translations of the *Bhagava Gita* and the *Upanishads*, learned the concepts of karma, reincarnation, maya (the illusion of this world), and the benefits of a vegetarian diet. Reincarnation made sense to me. How could we be expected to get it right in just one lifetime?

While there are numerous Hindu sects with an array of beliefs, my understanding from this particular sect was that there is one Supreme Being, a creator God called Brahman, who manifests himself in different forms as gods and goddesses. This is, by no stretch of the imagination, idol worship. On the contrary, it is a complex belief system which views God as the one and the many, both at the same time. Each image is not the totality of God, but an aspect of God made manifest to help humans relate to divinity.

I was enjoying my experience with Hinduism. I loved dressing up in a colorful *sari*, feasting on delicious vegetarian food, and dancing with abandon in front of the altar as we sang in unison to the beat of drums, the ring of the cymbals, and the enchanting cry of the sitar. I felt elated, like the puffy fuzz of a dandelion floating in the breeze.

One spring afternoon at the temple, I joined two American devotees planting violet and yellow pansies in the courtyard. The woman said she wasn't feeling well and went upstairs to lie down. The man, her husband, followed her, a look of concern on his face. I continued digging and planting, enjoying the soft dirt on my hands, the warmth of the sun on my skin. Sparrows chirped in the trees and a yellow butterfly flitted about. While working on my row of pansies, I looked up and noticed the eight-foot walls surrounding the courtyard. Suddenly, my heart constricted. The walls felt confining, suffocating. I could barely breathe. I got up, feeling compelled to get out of there.

I went inside and checked the lower level of the house. No one was around, so I assumed they'd all be in their bedrooms upstairs and did not want to disturb them. Throwing off the sari, I pulled on my pants and blouse and bolted out the front door, relieved to be in the open area of the street.

The following week, I went to the temple on Friday morning as usual. I was not greeted at the door or offered a sari. Everyone wore somber expressions. I wondered if someone had died.

"The head of the temple would like to speak to you," said the American devotee. I followed him to a private room where the Iranian accountant sat in his white cotton clothes, his expression grave.

"I was informed that you left the temple last week without telling anyone." He shifted uncomfortably.

"That's true. I was outside and just started feeling all weird like I couldn't breathe. I needed to just get out into the open air and no one was downstairs, so I left."

"There were other devotees upstairs," he said slowly, looking into my eyes.

"I know, but…"

"There are no buts. I am your teacher, your *guru*. As a devotee, you must have complete devotion, surrender, and obedience. That means that you do not eat or sleep or even drink water without my permission, much less just get up and leave whenever it pleases you."

Saying I was shocked would be an understatement. I felt numb and nauseated and furious all at the same time. I had already had my fill of limitations placed on me by the mere fact of being a woman in Iran. My college classes and my job had granted me a much-coveted freedom to at least make some of my own choices and to come and go as I pleased, a freedom I had not enjoyed in high school. *No one* was going to take that away from me.

The silence hung between us, thick and heavy. My hands curled into fists; my fingernails drew blood from my palms. Heat rose to my head and spread across my face. I narrowed my eyes and fixed him with a smoldering gaze. His sober expression of superiority shifted, softened.

Without another word, I turned on my heel and stormed out the door, slamming it hard in my wake. The vibrations of metal and glass spread through the house.

BUDDHISM

In my mid-twenties, I returned to America and began working toward a degree in English at San Diego State University. During my second semester, I signed up for a course in world religions. The year was 1977. The professor, blond hair hanging down to his shoulders, wore a colorful, oversized shirt, wooden beads, a straw hat, and leather sandals. At the beginning of each class, he sat cross-legged on his desk and we all chanted "OM" for a few minutes before beginning the lecture. Used to the conservative teachers in Iran, I found this eclectic man refreshing. I liked the sensations the "OM" chant produced: a vibration that spread down to my bones.

The professor seemed well-versed in his subject matter. He could even read Sanskrit. I had spent my last few years in Iran in a spiritual limbo, so now I welcomed the opportunity to learn more about spirituality, to help quench that undying thirst that burned inside me..

Mid-semester, the professor introduced Buddhism. Buddhists believe that suffering arises from attachment to desires. Freedom from suffering can be achieved by following the Eightfold Path, three of which are Right Thought, Right Speech, and Right Action—similar to Zoroastrian beliefs. *Interesting.*

I learned about the wheel of *karma* and the goal of pursuing a state of enlightenment or *Nirvana*. Buddhism has no supreme deity and no dogma; there are no "absolutes" in Buddhism. All teachings and beliefs are designed to get you where you need to go and then be discarded.

We watched a video that portrayed a river made of light and matter. The narrator talked about how human beings are part of one continuous flow of life and that the separation we experience is an illusion. My stomach knotted. How could I be one with everything else? *I* was an *individual*-- special, separate, unique! I did not care for this video. I did not like these ideas.

I was assigned to read a book about Zen Buddhism. Each time I picked it up, I fell asleep after reading a few pages. At other times, I'd feel a stab of anxiety in my gut. A part of me, perhaps the ego, did not want me to learn about oneness. My ego insisted that I hold to the idea that I was separate and *it* was in charge of my life.

I trudged through the book as if I were walking through a tar pit and barely completed the class.

SHAMANISM

In the summer of 1978, I registered for an anthropology class titled "Magic and Mysticism." The professor, a bulky man with stringy sun-bleached hair and piercing eyes, had worked as a field anthropologist, visiting many indigenous peoples. He had studied their concepts of spirituality and learned from the *shaman* of the tribes.

He stood behind the podium, arms crossed. His tribal shirt looked Peruvian.

"The *shaman*," he said, leaning forward, "were the healers and spiritual teachers of the tribe."

Images of old black and white movies with strange-looking African witch doctors flickered through my mind.

"The shaman did not *believe* in a spiritual world." The professor paused, scanning us for our reactions. The room was still; all eyes glued on this charismatic man. "He *experienced* spirituality by going into altered states and journeying into the spiritual realm."

I sat up straight, ears perked.

"The shaman became the link for his people, the link between the physical and spiritual worlds. Here, you will see examples of shamans in action." The lights dimmed, the sound of beating drums filled the room, and the images of shamanic ceremonies from Siberia, Africa, and Mexico appeared on the movie screen.

The old movie images of witch doctors dissipated as I soaked up this new concept—the *direct experience* of spirituality. Up to this point, everything I had learned about God and spirituality required *faith* and *belief*. Shamanism was *experience*.

One of the assigned books was *Tales of Power* by Carlos Castaneda. Captivated, I could barely put the book down. This book *talked* to me, resonated with something deep inside. Instead of being at the mercy of a judgmental God who punished you severely and possibly through all eternity if you didn't follow his specific rules, Carlos and his teacher, Don Juan, spoke of personal power, of choices, of freedom, of the ability to *change* your reality. This was new information—wonderful, magical.

After the semester ended, I purchased other books by Castaneda: *The Teachings of Don Juan, A Separate Reality,* and *Journey to Ixtlan*, devouring the material as if I had been hungry for my entire life and was suddenly presented with real food.

It was early 1979. I had just completed Castenada's newest book, *The Second Ring of Power.* His later books had not yet been published. The wonderful, delicious, mysterious food was gone. I was empty, lost. I did not know where to go or how to seek further information.

The candle flame flickered in the dark room, casting shadows on the wall. Sitting cross-legged on the bare floor in our San Diego duplex, I lit an incense stick and watched the swirls of smoke in the dim light. I could sense a deep mystery calling to me, its pull so strong that my soul ached, but I didn't know how to answer the call. No religion I had encountered spoke to me. I sat staring at the candle flame, feeling helpless and confused.

A loud knock jerked me back to reality. "What are you doing in there?" my husband, Bahman, yelled from behind the door as if I were hard of hearing. I didn't remember locking the door. "What's for dinner?" he added, sounding slightly perturbed.

My mind flooded with things I needed to do, ordinary things, everyday things. Complete assignment for a class, take inventory at work, pick up groceries, go to the laundromat, prepare dinner…

Blowing out the candle, I rose and left the room. Life was busy, demanding. Spirituality would have to wait.

Making Sense of It All

I knew I'd barely touched these many religions, yet none of them resonated with me, none had called me to go deeper, to learn more. I found myself with many more questions than answers. Many people believe in a supreme creator: Brahman, Yahwah, God, Allah, The Great Spirit, Ahura Mazda…., but did the name really matter? Did using *different* names make God a different God? Or was the person's *intent*, what they actually felt, what they really meant, was what mattered?

People demonstrate their theology in different forms. Some forms of worship are serious and sober, like the Catholic mass or the Moslem prayer. Some rituals are quiet and contemplative like the Buddhist meditation; others are joyful like the Hindu chants and dances. If God is omniscient, all-knowing, all powerful, why would he care what *form* of devotion or worship or prayer people used? Wouldn't the end result be more important than the means?

Was God formless as Moslems proclaimed, or could God also take forms such as Jesus and Krishna? Wouldn't an omnipotent God be able to do both?

Were we powerless beings destined to live in fear of eternal damnation from an almighty God, or were the teachings of Don Juan Matus and the shamans of indigenous tribes the real truth? With direct experience of God, we would not need doctrine and dogma. We would not need to have faith or belief. The *experience* would speak for itself.

Finding no clear answers, I became an agnostic.

Chapter Two: The Wake-up Call

An easy life doesn't teach us anything. In the end, it's learning that matters; what we've learned and how we've grown.

-Richard Bach

San Diego, California - 1979

"This form of cancer is unusual for a woman of twenty-eight." The doctor's words hung heavy in the air. He shuffled papers, his eyes averted. Bahman sat transfixed to the adjacent chair, gulping air furiously.

I was twenty-one when I met Bahman. We'd been English teachers at the Imperial Air Force in Tehran. He was a soft-spoken, gentle Iranian—the type of man who made you feel safe. Chestnut hair tumbling down to his shoulders framed fair skin and exotic dark chocolate eyes. Studying in Berkeley, California, in the late 'sixties,

Bahman had dived neck-deep in the Berkley counterculture—its long hair, music, psychedelic drugs, protests, sit-ins, demonstrations, UFO stories, government conspiracy theories, and fascination with Eastern philosophies including yoga, meditation, and vegetarianism. He'd done it all. Starving to experience life after years of a sheltered existence in Iran, I had gravitated to Bahman as if I'd been lost in the desert and had stumbled upon an oasis.

Back in Tehran, we used to hang out with a group of English teachers from work. Gathered in the courtyard of a colleague's home, we listened to Bahman tell stories of his Berkeley adventures:

"It was about 1969 and he University of California had bulldozed a series of student houses on Haste Street near Telegraph Avenue. They wanted to make it into a parking lot." His eyes flashed and his usual smile grew grim. "People were furious. They protested, got together in meetings, talked to the local merchants and agreed to make it into a community park – *the People's Park.*"

The Iranians listened, wide-eyed. The Americans nodded. They'd heard of this event.

"We all got together, hundreds of people clearing the ground, planting trees and flowers and grass. We set up playground equipment. Even made a sandbox. People handed out free food. You had to be there – we all felt like we were doing something good, something for the community. It was exhilarating."

I listened with rapt attention. Telling these stories, Bahman was no longer just the soft-spoken English teacher. I began to see him with new eyes.

"A few weeks later, the university decided it wanted its land back. They bulldozed the gardens and began putting up a fence around the park. People were outraged. A large crowd gathered to protest. The police fired tear gas. We threw rocks at them. They began shooting. One guy was blinded, another killed. Lots of people were injured. Then the National Guard showed up in full battle gear and things got really scary, but people kept protesting anyway."

Bahman paused to sip Coca Cola from a bottle; his audience silent, waiting. I watched him with wide eyes, helplessly seduced by his charm and worldly experiences.

"Finally the university decided to lease the park to the city. We gathered in huge crowds, thousands of us, showing the peace sign to the police and guards." Bahman demonstrated the peace sign for all to see.

"Did it become a park?" asked a pixie-faced young woman.

"It took a while, but I've heard from friends that it's now a park – People's Park."

* * * * *

In 1974, Bahman sent his parents to ask for my hand in marriage, the way it's done in Iran. I was twenty-three on my wedding day, facing an endless line of relatives planting wet kisses first on one cheek, then the other. Hips swayed and feet drummed to the beat of popular Persian music. Guests sipped aromatic Darjeeling tea from dainty glasses and munched on tiny cookies made of chick pea flour shaped like a summer bloom and honey-dripped baklavas stuffed with pistachios. Aromas of lamb and saffron and buttered basmati rice drifted from the adjacent kitchen.

I sensed the warmth of Bahman's hand on mine as we proudly perched on the blue velvet couch and greeted the guests as if we were holding court. Bahman – my new husband! I felt as giddy as a teenager trying to digest it all. Life was so delicious. I was loved. I was married. Everything from now on was going to be just wonderful.

In 1977, after completing his military service, Bahman and I returned to the states to continue our education— I'd dropped out of college after we married. We'd always dreamed of having children, imagining little versions of ourselves running around the house. I'd even believed I was pregnant once – just a few months after our wedding. We both liked to lay hands on my belly, in awe of the little being growing inside. Our bubble burst when pregnancy test results were negative and I had to have a shot to get my period started again. Five years later, I'd finally questioned my doctor why I hadn't conceived. The doctor ordered a D and C, a scraping of the lining of the uterus. The procedure had revealed the cancer.

The doctor rose, extending his hand. "Try not to worry. You'll be receiving the best treatment available."

Back in our duplex, Bahman perched on the side of the bed; he looked haggard, spent. He played with his moustache, pulling and twisting the hairs on one side.

"What are we going to do?" he said, his voice constricted.

"I'll have the operation and see what happens. What choice do I have?"

"I know, I know." His face paled. "I mean, if you take two months off from work, how are we going to live?"

I gawked at him incredulously. We were college students with part-time jobs. Both paychecks were needed to cover rent, bills, food. "I guess I'll have to call my father in Iran," I replied, feeling queasy inside. I would have to swallow my pride in order to ask my father for help, knowing he had more than his share of problems with the chaos following the 1979 Iranian revolution.

Bahman's demeanor brightened. He patted me on the back and went out to get us something to eat.

I lit a tapered candle on the nightstand, staring blankly at the flickering flame, sensing a pull, a calling to something ethereal, intangible. Something beyond my comprehension or understanding. Inside, I'm a gaping hole begging to be filled, yet I have no religion or tradition, nothing to grasp, nowhere to turn. To me, organized religion is God packaged neatly in a box and ingeniously marketed. I watch the shadows dance on the wall, wondering if there's something else out there, a spiritual belief that makes sense to me. I know "God-in-the-box" will never work for me.

I breathe in short gasps. I'm only twenty eight years old. How can my life be over when it's barely begun? I want to finish my degree and go on to graduate school. I thought I would have children, or at least one, and really be there for her, be a good mom so she'd never ever feel alone. And I've always wanted a house. A place I could plant roots and call my own. I thought I'd travel with my husband to far, exotic places--stroll warm sandy beaches on tropical islands and swim the Great Barrier Reef. I'd always imagined taking photos at the Egyptian Pyramids, the Great Wall of China, and the Eiffel Tower. I believed that, maybe, one day I would even become a writer and people all over the world would read my books.

In reality, I have been trudging through life with a fake façade, as if I had no problems, as if everything were okay, hoping that if I stuck my head in the sand, my fears and problems would simply vanish. Now, face to face with death, I'm toppled headlong into an abyss, arms and legs flailing, finding no one with the strength to support me, believing in no deity that could protect or save me.

I find myself forced to look, to examine my life with brutal honesty. I've done nothing that really matters. I've helped no one; made no contribution to society; created nothing of significance. My life boils down to working, going to school, eating, sleeping, watching TV, reading novels, with an occasional gathering of family and friends—a constant struggle for survival interspersed with cheap distractions to help me forget, to let me escape for a while. I find no meaning, no purpose to my life, only emptiness. I have not lived; I've only existed. I could die today and easily be forgotten as if I never was. My forehead breaks out into a cold sweat as I'm faced with the grim reality:

My life makes no difference in the world.

THE OPERATION

I sat on a hospital bed shivering in a thin white gown, slapping my thighs to an imagined tune. A blonde nurse with glasses too big for her face grabbed my arm and stuck it with a needle. She looked me in the eyes and beamed a smile. "This will make you feel better."

Lying flat on the bed, I studied the cracks in the ceiling as the morphine coursed through my veins. *If I make it through this, I'm going to make changes, turn my life around. There has to be some meaning to life; otherwise, what's the point?* A loudspeaker paged Doctor Richards. An ambulance siren screamed in the distance. I took a deep breath. *If you really do exist, God, I could use some help just about now.* The ceiling cracks began to blur and the knot in my stomach softened as the morphine took hold. I felt light and at ease.

A lithe orderly with short-cropped hair moved me from my bed to a gurney.

"Would you like to see how fast this thing can go?" He flashed a set of brilliant white teeth.

I thought about how funny people looked upside down. "Okay."

The gurney took off with a jerk. We raced down hallways and skidded around corners of Kaiser Hospital—our laughter echoing through the stark, long corridors. The orderly slowed down as we approached the operating area. I wiped the tears of laughter from my eyes.

"Fear not," said a voice. I raised my head and scanned the area. No one other than the orderly was in sight. "You will be fine," said the voice, its tone like a temple chime.

Maybe it's the drugs.

The orderly parked me near the wall. "I'll be back in a flash." His olive skin gleamed in the fluorescent light. I watched him as he disappeared behind the double doors of the operating room.

My skin tingled. A current snaked down my spine and spread through my body. My arms blossomed with goose bumps.

"You have nothing to worry about," said the voice, like the tinkling of a wind chime in a soft summer breeze. "Everything will turn out just fine." Delicious warmth enveloped my heart and radiated out to my limbs.

As the orderly rolled me into the operating room, I craned my neck and searched the hallway.

* * * * *

Raising his head from examining the suture, the doctor gave me a thumbs-up. "Fortunately, we discovered it early enough and got it all." He grinned with satisfaction. I realized the implication that he didn't always get it all.

"You won't need any chemotherapy." The doctor disappeared behind the curtains like a magician in a stage show.

I flipped the channels with the remote: a talk show about lesbians, "CHIPS," the news, a rerun of "Star Trek"…

I clicked off the TV and lay back in the bed. *I'm okay.* I sighed, recalling my prayer for help. *Did God help me or did I just get lucky?*

A ray of sunlight stretched across the bed. I peered out the window to a patch of turquoise sky decorated with a candy cotton cloud. I had been given a second chance. I wasn't sure exactly how, but things were going to change.

I sat up straight, with deliberation and resolve. Hands and eyes raised to the heavens, I declared out loud: "God, Spirit, Higher Power, whomever or whatever you are, if you *are* out there, hear me now. Help me find purpose and meaning to my life. Help me find my way."

* * * * *

When I was dismissed from the hospital, Bahman took me home and helped me into bed. I felt woozy from the drugs.

"Are you all right?"

"I guess."

"Okay. I'm going out to play volleyball with the guys." He planted a kiss on my cheek and slipped out the door.

The gaping chasm inside me grew and grew. I was alone. So very alone…

* * * * *

Two months after the operation, I returned to work.

"You've been transferred to a new department," said the store manager, fumbling with papers on his desk. "Jared will be your new department manager." He rose, indicating my appointment time had concluded. A quick, firm handshake, and I was out the door.

Jared, tall and lithe with strawberry blonde hair, was with a customer when I approached the jewelry department. He gently clasped a diamond-studded bracelet around a middle-aged woman's wrist. "Looks fabulous," he said, picking up her hand so that the diamonds sparkled in the light.. "Like it was made just for you." The customer turned her chubby hand around to study it. A sudden gleam lit up her eyes. "I'll take it," she said, stretching out her wrist like a queen waiting for her attendants.

"You deserve it," Jared responded, gently unclasping the bracelet and placing it in a blue velvet box almost reverently. The stout woman giggled, then trailed off, looking elated with her purchase.

I stepped up to the counter and introduced myself.

"Well, I'm delighted that you'll be joining us, Ms. Patricia," he exclaimed in a southern drawl as he warmly shook my hand.

* * * * *

In the small enclosure of the jewelry department, I experienced the same feelings I'd had when I lived in Iran with its tall, confining walls. The store expected me to stand there, like a guardsman at a sultan's vault, watching over their precious gems. I couldn't even go to the bathroom unless another employee took my place. *Just a while longer until I get my baccalaureate degree. Then I'm out of here.* A customer stepped up to the counter. I faked a smile.

"Why don't you take a break," Jared tapped my shoulder. "You look like you need one." I grabbed the see-through plastic purse that all employees were required to use, and beat a hasty retreat.

Jared was a personable man with a bright disposition— a gentle soul with an infectious smile. I enjoyed his company. He was easy to talk to and he laughed a lot. His presence made the agony of forced politeness with obnoxious customers bearable-- almost.

Jared loved to talk about the minister of his church, especially on Mondays after he'd been inspired by her the previous day. I had a picture of church engraved in my head from my childhood and believed that all organizations with the title "church" would be similar in nature. Like a magic word, Jared would say "church," and my ears would close down and a veritable fortress would pop up around me, although I smiled politely and nodded as he spoke.

Then, one day, Jared invited me to visit his church. Red lights flashed behind my eyes. My brain screamed: "Red alert! Red alert!" Heat flushed my face.

"It's not a regular church. It's different. Fun."

I wasn't buying. "Isn't it a *Christian* church?"

"No, it's non-denominational."

"What does that mean?"

"It means they accept and honor the teachings of all the great masters like Jesus *and* Buddha."

I refused to budge. "Church" conjured up images of dark-robed priests instilling the fear of God in their flock; of solemn people dressed in their Sunday best, eyes lowered, guilt written all over their faces. But Jared was relentless, especially when talking about his minister. "She says you can have *anything* you want in your life," he gesticulated with enthusiasm. "This is not like other churches. It's very different, even entertaining. Come and see for yourself."

I stuck to my guns.

As the months passed and our friendship evolved, he chipped away at my defensive armor.

In the spring of 1980, he invited me and a Japanese woman who worked with us to join him for a Sunday service followed by brunch. "And bring your husbands, too."

I had no intention of going to church and was working on an excuse so as not to hurt Jared's feelings when the Japanese woman showed up to begin her shift.

"My husband said okay. We're going," she said as she placed her sweater and see-through purse under the counter.

I glanced at her, then at Jared, feeling like a trapped animal.

"Come on, Patricia! We'll go as a group. It'll be a blast." He draped one arm across my shoulders.

"I'll talk to Bahman tonight." I thought it was a safe bet that my husband, raised a Moslem, would refuse. To my shock and disbelief, he actually agreed to go. He thought it would be "an experience."

At the time, it did not occur to me that this might be an answer to my plea for help on the hospital bed. The church was the La Jolla Church of Religious Science. The minister's name was Terry Cole-Whittaker.

The service was held at the historic El Cortez Hotel in downtown San Diego. The minister, an attractive blonde dressed in a cream-colored outfit with matching shoes burst onto the stage to enthusiastic applause.

Music filled the room. People rose and milled about, singing about reaching out and touching and making the world a better place. The theatre came alive with greetings, handshakes, and hugs. No bloody Jesus hanging on the cross, no hardened priests admonishing people to repent, no nuns with permanent scowls etched on their faces. No *guilt*. This was definitely not my vision of "church."

The congregation returned to their seats and settled down.

"What does your life look like right now?" Terry scanned the upturned faces.

Not too hot.

She paced the stage, paused, turned to face us. "Is your life what you want it to be?"

"Nooooo," replied the congregation in unison.

"Do you want change?"

"Yes!" Their voices roared.

I wanted change, I wanted it so bad it hurt, but my skeptical mind was in full gear: *What is this religion? What are they really about?*

Terry paced the stage again, then suddenly stopped and looked straight at the congregation, pointing her finger. "YOU have the power to make that change." Loud applause, cheers, whistles. Terry's eyes were on fire.

I glanced at Bahman sitting next to me, his face emotionless, complacent. I recalled the adventurous rebel I'd fallen in love with: we'd hiked the mountains in northern Tehran, listened to tapes of Donovan and Elton John, visited the first pizza parlor in Iran, explored Hinduism at an underground temple practicing yoga, chants, and, for a brief interlude, we became vegetarians. Friendship blossomed into love. We were young when we married-- I was 23, he was 26--we were in love, and the world was a blank page full of possibilities. But Bahman had changed over the years, becoming more conservative, more complacent. Nowadays, he loved taking trips to Las Vegas, playing volleyball or cards, or just hanging out with his buddies. Over time, he'd become less willing to try new things, explore new places, learn and change and grow.

The minister's voice pulled me back. "Let's take a look at what you want to create, what you want to know, what you want to be. With God, all things are possible."

With God? Is God real? Well, I DID survive the cancer, but...

"It's all about consciousness. It's all about belief. If you have the consciousness that it's not spiritual to be abundant, that you don't deserve to be loved, to be happy--if you have the consciousness that you're a victim and there's nothing you can do to change anything, well, God just nods his head and says 'As you wish'."

She continued her talk. I glanced around the room. People perched on the edge of their seats, hanging on to her every word. They laughed, they wept, they watched, and they listened, mesmerized, charmed. *They look like they worship her. I don't know about this...*

In spite of my doubts, this charismatic woman had stirred something inside of me. My life was in a rut. Did I have the power to make the necessary changes? Folding my arms in front of me, I leaned back in my seat.

"We are each made in the image and likeness of God and we have the power to create. In this ministry, we believe in miracles. Yes!" Terry shot her fist up into the air. The audience exploded.

Musicians appeared on the stage and sang about finding the power within. We clapped and swayed and sang along. My exterior shell began to crack.

Just as the musicians retreated, angelic voices rose from the choir in the back of the theatre. The minister's words resonated in my head: *The power is within you.* At the same time, the voice of caution whispered in my ear: *Remember the Hindu temple in Tehran, how it stirred your soul, how good it felt, at least in the beginning. Remember how it turned out in the end.*

Terry stepped forward on the stage and asked everyone to stand up and hold hands. Jared grabbed my left hand, Bahman the right one. I fought my reluctance, let out a deep sigh, and joined with the musicians, the choir, the music blasting from loud speakers, and the entire congregation singing in one voice, hands clasped, swaying side to side, asking for peace on earth and accepting the responsibility that peace began with me.

"That was fun, wasn't it?" Jared asked as we weaved our way through the crowd. They seemed more animated now, filled with life.

"It was okay."

"Maybe we can do this again some time," he added, searching my face for signs of approval.

"Maybe."

Chapter Three: The Many Faces of the One

Each time you see or hear the word God, think of the person next to you, the family at work or at play, and the true essence of who you are at the core. Do not think of a singular power higher than yourself somewhere in the sky. It is you!

– Kryon

SUMMER 1983 – SAN DIEGO, CALIFORNIA

I'm thirty-two years old and my life has finally begun to stabilize. I've graduated from San Diego State University with a Masters degree in Linguistics. I no longer drudge through my workdays at the department store, but for two years now, I've been enjoying a stimulating job teaching ESL (English as a Second Language) and it pays three times as much as my sales job did. I drive a spiffy new Ford Escape, pearl white. Our apartment is larger than before, in a more upscale neighborhood with high beam ceilings and a wood fireplace. Bahman and my sister's husband have gone into business together managing a copy center. Every so often, we even take a vacation.

It's Saturday afternoon. Piles of my photographs sit on the dining table, sorted by different life periods. An old black and white picture grabs me: it's Ed and me when we were kids. Technically my uncle, Ed was more like a brother, only five years older than me.

When I was a little girl, I always loved hanging out with Ed. He was older. He knew stuff. He was someone I felt comfortable and safe with. We loved to watch scary movies together and share comic books and stroll up to the local Dairy Queen for chocolate-covered ice cream on a stick. Ed was someone I could talk to, someone I could trust, my mentor, my confidant, my best friend.

When I was nine, my mother took off with another man, so – just like that – my father had me yanked from my quiet suburban town in Elyria, Ohio and sent me half a world away to Tehran. No more America, no more Halloween costumes or Christmas trees or Easter baskets, no more fireworks on the Fourth of July, and no more Ed.

The last time I'd seen Ed, he was fourteen and had come to say goodbye. He crouched down to my height, gripping my arms. "Do you understand that we may never see each other again?" He shaked me slightly, his eyes filled with pain. I stared at him and nodded. He enveloped me in a warm embrace, lingered, then pulled back and handed me a batch of comic books to read on the plane. "Thanks." I ran one finger over the cover of *Wonder Woman*. Ed turned one last time before stepping out the door. I waved goodbye with a stony face, then jumped up on the couch to watch him through the window. Wiping an escaped tear with the back of my hand, I turned to watch a cartoon on TV.

Back in my San Diego apartment, I examine the photograph. I was three and Ed was eight. He was kneeling on the grass petting the dog, while I gazed at him with admiration, a huge grin on my face. Our families lived next door in New Jersey back then.

One hot afternoon, about the same time period, I was cranky and hot. Ed tied a couple of washrags together to make me a bathing suit, then filled a bucket with cool water. "Get in here. This should cool you off." He patted my back, gently pushing me towards the bucket.

I found Ed's broad smile reassuring, so I plopped down into the bucket, bottom first, my short legs sticking straight up in the air. Water splashed every which way.

"Ed, I can't get out!"

Ed was bent over, holding his sides, laughing so hard he couldn't talk. Tears streaked his face.

"Ed! Get me out!"

Tall and broad shouldered, even at eight, he gently lifted me out of the bucket, wrapped me in a large towel, and carried me into the house. I leaned my head against his chest feeling protected and safe and secure. This is the first memory of my life.

* * * * *

In early fall, just a few months after reminiscing about Ed, I got a phone call from Nana who now lived in Florida.

"Patsy? You're not going to believe this."

"Nana? Hi! How've you been?"

"He called me, Patsy. Can you believe it? Ed. He called me!"

My heart skipped a beat

"After all these years," she sighed. "I didn't even know where he was."

"Where is he?"

"San Francisco. And he said he's coming. Here. Can you believe it?" Nana sounded more excited than she'd been in years.

Images of my childhood mentor and friend raced through my mind: Ed makes me a Halloween costume and dresses me up so I look like George Washington. We're soaping the windows of a neighbor's house because the porch lights are off—they're too stingy to hand out candy. A woman swings open the door and screams, shaking her finger. Scrambling down the street like Jack the Ripper is after us, we hide behind a house and laugh so hard our sides ache.

Later that year, it's winter, cold, the yard covered in snow. We pile onto Ed's sled, squealing with laughter as his dog, Pepper, hauls us down the frozen river bed.

The adventures never cease. It's midnight on a starry summer eve. We sneak up to the local graveyard to see if the ghosts of the dead really come out. A gate creaks and blows shut in the wind. Screaming with terror, we fly down the street, tear across the back yard, and burst into the kitchen to the horrified faces of our parents who believe us to be in bed.

I'm eight years old and in the hospital to have my tonsils removed, feeling lonely and glum. Suddenly, Ed's face appears in the window, his arms piled high with

Superman and *Wonder Woman* comic books. He brings tickles and giggles and piggyback rides all around the hospital ward.

Nana's voice brings me back to San Diego. "How old do you think he is now?"

"I'm thirty-two, Nana, so Ed should be thirty-seven."

"Oh my, he's a grown man." She pauses, sighs. "Did I ever tell you about the time I took the train up to Canada and came back with a cute little baby boy? He had a full head of dark hair."

I'd heard the story of Ed's adoption numerous times. My mother had been an only child, but Nana had wanted another, so she adopted Ed from Canada. My mother was thirteen at the time.

"You know, Patsy, after I married Bob, I came back for him. I was going to take him with me." Her voice was more solemn now. "But he never wanted to see me. Every time I came to the house, he'd run out the back door."

I knew that story, too. Back in the fifties, when Ed was twelve years old, Nana had gotten fed up with Papa. For years, he'd been a heavy drinker and an insufferable womanizer. There'd been a scene in the airport, with Papa begging her to stay but Nana refusing to relent. A navy man in New Jersey loved her, she said. He'd proposed. She'd have a better life with him.

Through all of that, Ed had watched, standing on the sidelines like a sack of potatoes, ignored and forgotten by both parents. He'd stayed with his father, who'd then married his childhood sweetheart, Maggie — a simple, kind, and gentle woman whom we all loved. About a year later, Papa died of a heart attack, leaving Ed with Maggie, his stepmother.

For all those years, Ed had borne the resentment of his mother's abandonment like an open wound. A few months after the divorce, Nana had tried to reconcile with him, but Ed had refused to see her or even talk about her. "Let's not talk of Madam," he would say to me.

Now he was returning, like the prodigal son, ready to heal, ready to forgive.

I'd had to grow up without my mother in Iran, so I understood. I knew how he must have felt, how hurt he must have been, even more so for being abandoned three times - first by his birth parents, then by his adopted mother, and finally by his father's death.

Nana's voice prodded me back to the present. "Patsy, are you there?"

"When does he plan to visit?"

"Thanksgiving weekend."

"I'm coming too, Nana. See you then."

November 1983, Florida

Nana met me at the gate in Miami Airport. I kept to her slow pace, holding on to her arm as we made our way through the bustling walkways to meet Ed, who was arriving on another flight. Pain was evident in Nana's face. I wasn't sure if it was due to the stress of the long walk or the guilt of what she had done those long years ago.

My heart raced as we approached Ed's gate. *I can't believe it's been twenty-four years since I last saw him.* I wondered what he looked like, what kind of person he had become. *Will he be the same, fun loving Ed? Will he still care about me?* I wiped sweaty hands on my skirt and glanced at Nana. Her face was tight, pinched. She panted from the long walk, too much for her overweight body to bear.

We searched the streams of travelers exiting the plane, wondering if we would recognize him. *He used to be big and tall with dark hair and glasses.*

A tall man walked straight up to us, green eyes laughing. "I thought I'd recognize you two," Ed said, his face breaking into a broad smile. His hair was lighter now, his expression more serious, more severe, as if life had not been kind to him. He did not wear glasses anymore.

I smiled up at him, feeling like a little girl. "I wasn't sure you would, since last time you saw me, I was only nine."

"You haven't grown much since then," he chuckled.

I punched him in the arm and giggled. It was good to see Ed again.

THE SHELL CRACKS

The following evening at dinner, Ed broached the painful subject. "Mom, I was really hurt when you left."

"Would you like some more gravy for your mashed potatoes, Ed?" Nana spooned the dark liquid onto his plate, without waiting for a response. "And I've got chocolate ice cream for dessert," she added, disappearing into the kitchen. Ed gave me a knowing look. My grandmother wasn't ready to tackle deep emotional issues. Maybe she couldn't handle the emotions; maybe it was the guilt. Maybe it was just the way of her generation—shove everything under the rug and act like it doesn't exist. While I believed it was horrible the way she had treated Ed those many years ago, she had always been kind to me and I loved her. I decided to stay clear of the whole mess and let them work it out.

After dinner, Ed and I took a long walk around the neighborhood.

"Don't hate your mother," he said, remembering his deceased sister. "She was a simple soul."

I became silent. My mother was not an issue I wanted to bring up. She had died when I was still in Iran. I remembered hearing the news while standing near the kitchen stove at our house in Tehran. I remembered shoving down the emotions that were fighting to surface while my younger sister cried. "She's so cold," my Iranian relatives said, shaking their heads, "Her mother just died and not a single tear. The girl is cold as ice."

A soft Florida rain began to fall as we turned a corner.

"She was still in school, a girl's school actually, when she met your father. Do you know the story?"

"Vaguely. Daddy never talked about her after she left." A part of me had disowned Mommy, but another part had clung to her memory, wishing Daddy would talk about her, remind me of her, make her alive again, make her real.

We pressed on down the sidewalk. The street lamps came on and lit up the rain.

"We lived in New Jersey back then. She was on a field trip to the Natural History Museum in New York with her class. Your father was studying architecture at Columbia University and visiting the museum at the same time." He smiled at the thought. "After they met, Mom wouldn't let them go on a date on their own. She chaperoned them everywhere they went."

Although talking about my mother stung, in spite of the inner pain, I chuckled at the image of Nana sitting in the back of the car, watching my parents with eagle eyes. I'd seen a photograph of Daddy when he was in college—think George Clooney in his twenties. No wonder Mommy had fallen for him.

The rain stopped abruptly. We headed back towards Nana's house.

Ed went on. "She was only seventeen when she married your father; eighteen when you were born. She was still a kid, a naïve one at that."

I tried to keep up with Ed's long gait, finding no words to respond. While I wanted to clap my hands over my ears—don't talk about my mother, it's too painful!—I found myself unable to shut out Ed's voice.

"She was scared." Ed's voice was sad, concerned. "She didn't know anything about Iran. She freaked out and ran."

I nodded, feigning understanding, my chest squeezing, tightening. It was Mommy's fault that I ended up in Iran, alone and motherless. It was all her fault.

"She never had a happy life, you know. She was only forty when she died."

I pondered this. Here was my uncle and best friend, come back after all these years to work out his own issues with my grandmother, and he was asking me to forgive my mother, his only sister. I hadn't thought about my mother for years. We'd both been abandoned, Ed and I. Maybe he was ready to confront his pain, ready to heal, but I didn't want to think about my mother, think about what my life would have been like if she'd never left. I wasn't ready to confront that issue. Wasn't sure I'd ever be ready.

* * * * *

The morning of our departure, my stomach contracted into a tight ball. Ed had somehow brought my childhood back to life—had connected me to that part of myself I had denied. I had abandoned that little girl when I left America and my closest friend, Ed. Somehow, in my psyche, the two had become intertwined. I boarded the plane with feelings of a cold fist closing over my heart. I held back the tears, stuffed the emotions fighting to surface, and held myself together using every shred of willpower I could muster.

Later that evening, I reached my apartment in San Diego and opened the suitcase to unpack. Without warning, my legs gave way and I collapsed on the floor, sobbing uncontrollably while a torrent of suppressed feelings and childhood pain erupted and poured out of me. Hours later, my husband, Bahman, found me lying on the floor, my body locked into fetal position, my eyes a vacant stare. He sat by me, helpless, lost—I had been the strong one in the relationship. I had always been the rock. He couldn't handle this—didn't handle this. I was on my own.

The next six months were a living hell. While I still had to get up each day, get dressed, teach my classes, pick up the groceries, prepare dinner… emotions welled up and churned inside of me—the pain unbearable, confusing. It just didn't make sense. Bahman and I got along just fine. No major financial problems. No health problems since the cancer operation. No issues at work. *What the hell is wrong with me?*

Tears would swell up for no apparent reason, at the most inopportune times—in the classroom where I was teaching, at the store when I was paying for my groceries, at the doctor's office for a routine check-up. I was embarrassed, confused, *angry* that I couldn't get a grip on these feelings. I had always been able to handle what life dealt me. I expected more from myself. My only solace was talking to Ed, because all this pain was connected to him. Only he could calm me, soothe me for a while, or so I believed. We visited each other a few times-- his home in San Francisco was only a short plane ride away—and talked frequently on the phone. We reminisced about our childhood, chatted about our current lives, and shared our dreams and aspirations. As my emotional turmoil intensified, I called him more and more often until it became a daily routine.

One day, he finally laid it on the line: "I think you need professional help."

Me! Professional help? I reeled at the thought.

The car skidded as I pulled out of my apartment parking lot and barreled down the road. *How dare he!* I slammed my fist on the steering wheel. *There is nothing wrong with me. I just like to talk to him, that's all.* A white Toyota pulled in front of me without signaling. I slammed the brakes to slow down and banged the horn. *Idiot!*

I turned towards Balboa Park, a place that always soothed me. After parking the car, I wandered aimlessly for over an hour, tears streaking my face. *I'm not crazy. Just a little sad, that's all. See a professional—where does he get this stuff?* It was a pleasant fall day and people milled about the gardens and strolled in and out of the museums. Children carried bright, colored balloons. A mime stood motionless on a corner. A street musician played a cheerful tune on a flute.

I found my way into the arboretum and sat on a ledge surrounded by tropical flowers. A waterfall splashed into a pond. I stretched out my legs and took several deep breaths. Painful as it was, I finally had to admit to myself that Ed was right. I needed help.

* * * * *

My quest for spirituality was on hold for the moment, so I went along with Ed's suggestion and sought traditional therapy. The opportunity to talk about my pain was welcome, but it didn't help much. It was too slow, too ineffective. After several months of therapy with no relief, I cried out to the heavens for help.

The following morning, I woke to find images of Terry Cole-Whittaker and the La Jolla Church of Religious Science dancing through my head. When I was working at the department store, I'd attended Terry's church each Easter with my department manager and other friends. That tradition had ended, however, when I quit the sales job and began teaching. I recalled the good feelings of the church, the powerful message. While I wasn't sure about the whole "church" thing, I was at the end of my rope. *Maybe* I could find some answers there.

Services moved between the El Cortez and the California hotels, so I had to pay attention in order to show up at the right place. I attended Terry's sermons every Sunday, listening, searching, groping for something that would help me deal with my inner pain. Attending church gave me some relief, albeit short-lived. I kept going back for more.

A few months later, on a fateful Sunday morning in 1984, a more solemn Terry Cole-Whittaker, just back from a trip to India, stepped onto the stage. She began her talk by sharing experiences from her recent travels.

"I saw people so poor you couldn't even imagine it," she said, less animated than during her previous sermons. "And even though they had close to nothing, they were *happy*." The congregation was suddenly still. I wondered if many of them had sought happiness in material wealth.

"These are the people we have been trying to save," she added, pacing across the stage. She stopped abruptly and faced the audience, eyes blazing: "Guess what? They don't need saving. Save yourselves."

The room went so silent you could hear a pin drop. Then Terry dropped her next bomb: she was going to dissolve her church. Groans. Disbelief. Faces glazed with shock. A few people began to sob out loud.

My stomach clenched. I was unsure what to do as I weaved through a mass of stunned people. They clustered, some staring into thin air, others gesticulating wildly, voices high and hysterical. A lone figure stood to one side, tears streaking his young face.

I finally managed to escape the heart-wrenching spectacle at the El Cortez Hotel, tossed the pink church program on the passenger's seat, and climbed into my car. My forehead pressed on the steering wheel, I pondered my fate. *What am I going to do now?*

I finally sat up straight and reached over to buckle my seatbelt. The pink church program had flipped over, displaying names of the church practitioners. I remembered hearing announcements about Religious Science practitioners—people trained by the church who would give congregation members individual assistance. I wasn't exactly sure what a practitioner did, but one name in particular seemed to pop up and hit me in the face.

Later at home, I discussed this with my husband. Bahman fiddled with his mustache, pain evident in his chocolate brown eyes. The solid rock that had been his wife was dissolving into sand and he had no clue how to deal with it. He let out a deep sigh and raked his hand through his hair. "Maybe he can help you," he finally blurted out.

I battled with the idea for some time, staring at the phone, trying to convince myself to make the call. Taking a deep breath, I picked up the receiver and dialed. The practitioner's name was Chris.

Meeting Chris

Chris's place was one of a group of cottages clustered around a courtyard with grass and flowers and a water fountain with a soothing splash. I hesitated in front of his door, still unsure of myself. My stomach fluttered like a hummingbird caught in a trap. *What am I doing here? What is a practitioner, anyway?*

Gathering up my courage, I took a deep breath and knocked. The door swung open to reveal a tall, slender man, with light brown hair that looked like it had been shaved off and was just beginning to grow back. He had a dark tan and a boyish face with bright green eyes. I stretched out my hand. He pushed it away and wrapped his arms around me in a warm embrace. My stomach calmed and I stepped inside.

He pulled up a chair, crossed his long legs, and invited me to tell him what was bothering me. He gave me his full attention, appearing to be genuinely concerned. His cottage was sparse, yet clean, painted in soft beiges and pinks. Tiny white Christmas lights were stapled to the ceiling all around the room, providing a gentle, yet festive glow. After a few moments of fidgeting with the couch pillows, I opened up and spilled out my story with barely a pause to breathe.

He smiled, a kind and gentle smile that put me at ease. "I understand what things look like right now. What you are feeling. Now, tell me what you *want* to feel. What you *want* things to look like."

His comments took me by surprise. "Well, ah, I want the pain to go away."

"And..."

"I don't know—maybe see Ed more often."

"Do you *need* to see him more often?"

"Ah, well, I *want* to."

"And if you don't, what will happen?

"I'll feel sad. I'll feel hurt."

"What if we make the pain go away?"

Silence.

"If the pain goes away, will you need to see Ed more often? Can you accept that Ed loves you, that he is your uncle and your friend, regardless of how often you see or talk to him?"

"I guess."

"Okay, let's treat."

"Treat?"

"It's a form of prayer."

He leaned forward to grab my hands. I jerked back, startled by instincts I'd gained from living in a Moslem country for sixteen years. This was a strange man attempting to touch me, and we were alone in his house.

Chris looked at me with a disarming smile. His eyes crinkled softly. He gently picked up my hands again. Sensing no sexual energy in the room, I allowed him to hold my hands. He closed his eyes and began the prayer.

"I, Chris, and Patricia, accept that there is only one God and we are one with that God."

My eyes flew open. I had heard the "one God" idea before, but "we are one with God?" This concept took me back to my experience studying Buddhism.

"I, Chris, being one with God, speak my word knowing that my word is law in the universe…"

One with God? My word is law? What was all this about? How could his word be law?

Chris completed the prayer, declaring that my emotions are calm and I accept that my uncle loved me. He then released it into the universe for manifestation. *Manifestation?*

Chris later explained that this was called a Spiritual Mind Treatment, a form of prayer used by the Church of Religious Science and the teachings of Ernest Holmes to bring about changes in one's life. I felt calmer now. The inner pain had softened. Fighting back my lingering fears and concerns, I made another appointment for the following week. Chris scribbled several titles of books for me to read along with directions to a metaphysical bookstore where I could purchase them. *A metaphysical bookstore?*

Following Chris's directions, I drove over to Controversial Bookstore on University Avenue. As I stepped through the door, the heady scent of incense and the sounds of drums and sitar coming over the speakers reminded me of the Hindu temple in Tehran. A petite woman with dreamy eyes looked up from behind the counter. "Good afternoon. Let me know if you need any assistance." Her long, beaded earrings dangled as she spoke.

I thanked her with a brief nod of my head, then gazed up at wood and brass images of Buddha and Kwan Yin and ancient Hindu Goddesses as I padded into the aisle. I drew my fingers reverently across the spines of several books, intoxicated by this rare find. *How could I not have known such a place existed?* Here was a wealth of metaphysical and spiritual information at my fingertips, shelves and shelves of books--on every religion, every tradition, every belief system, old and new, alive or dead. There were books on self-help; books on healing; books on indigenous cultures from around the world. I saw books on crystals, astrology, numerology, near death experiences and the occult; books on magic, books on shamanism; books on everything and anything spiritual I could ever imagine or even dream of.

Like a ravenous tigress who had just stumbled upon food after a long stretch of hunger, I snatched books from various shelves. My heart drummed as I staggered to the front desk and dropped my pile of new-found treasures on the counter with a thump. Snapping up a box of incense from a counter-top display, I tossed it on top of the heap.

The petite woman looked up from behind the tall pile of books, amusement evident in her eyes. "Will this be all?"

Chris had recommended two books. I purchased a dozen, made my way home, and read and read. My mind stretched like a rubber band.

WE ARE ONE

My first visit to a metaphysical bookstore was only the beginning. I frequented Controversial Bookstore and other such shops in the San Diego area on a regular basis, reading every waking hour that my schedule permitted. My mind filled with a cornucopia of ideas, beliefs, and knowledge from numerous cultures, religions, and traditions. At first, everything was a jumble in my head, like a jigsaw puzzle not yet assembled. Yet, little by little, I began to notice patterns, threads of belief that flowed through various traditions. One such belief viewed God as imminent, a spiritual energy, a divine consciousness that permeates all of creation. While this concept was unfamiliar to me, it has been understood by mystics throughout the ages and has been a core belief of Eastern philosophies and indigenous religions for thousands of years. Consider:

- *Namaste* is a well-known greeting in India. It means *I honor the God in you*.

- The Huichol, an ancient tribe living in the Sierra Madre Mountains in Mexico, believe the "life force" or *kupuri* flows through all things – humans, plants, and animals. To the Huichol, all souls are one.

- Jesus of Nazareth said, "For as the body is one and hath many members, and all the members of that one body, being many, are one body: so also is Christ. For by one Spirit are we all baptized into one body whether we be Jews or Gentiles, whether we be bound or free, and have been all made to drink into one Spirit.

For the body is not one member, but many. If the foot shall say, Because I am not the hand, I am not of the body; is it therefore not of the body? And if the ear shall say, Because I am the eye; I am not the body; is it therefore not the body?" (I Cor. 12-16)

- In the *Ho'omana* teaching of Hawai'i, power emanates from the One, the source of all—all life, all energy.

- In Navajo philosophy, *Sa'a naghai bik'e hozho,* an energy, a force that created the universe, is in all things and connects all things.

- In the Yoruba tradition of West Africa, *Ase* is honored as the Universal Life Force, the unifying power that connects all life to the oneness of creation.

- Hildegard of Bingen, a twelfth century abbess and mystic said: "I, the fiery life of divine essence, am aflame beyond the beauty of the meadows, I gleam in the waters, and I burn in the sun, moon, and stars…I awaken everything to life."

- *Mitakuye Oyasin,* say the Lakota Sioux. We are all related.

This idea of God began to make sense to me. *It's like God is the ocean, and we're each a drop; God a body, and each of us a cell; God a sun, and each one of us a ray, or God-spark.* I started to realize that we are spirits in body form, eternal souls who choose to temporarily wear a human form and have human experiences. These human forms give us the illusion that we are each separate individuals, while our true identity is our spiritual forms, sparks of the Creator. In other words, we are all one--one with creation, one with each other, one with God. Believing that we are separate from God is like a cell in our pinky finger feeling separate from the body and getting depressed because it is all alone.

With all this information in so many diverse traditions and cultures referring to the oneness of divinity and *our being part of that oneness,* how did we ever get so confused? I wondered how the world would change, how *we* would change, if we all knew, not believed, but *knew,* felt it in the marrow of our bones, our very genes, that we, all of humanity, are the many faces of the One? That each person we encounter is a unique expression of divinity; that there is no "them" and "us"—there never was.

THE HEALING BEGINS

At the end of my next visit, Chris said: "We're having a group rebirthing this Saturday—up in La Jolla. You should come."

"What's rebirthing?"

"It's just a breathing process." He gestured with his hands for emphasis. Chris had a certain spark, an energy that was contagious.

I grimaced. What was this new weird thing he was talking about now? I was just getting comfortable with the Spiritual Mind Treatments. I wasn't sure I was ready for something new.

"It helps remove blocked emotions," he added with a disarming smile.

I crossed my arms. "I don't know…"

"It will be helpful to you. You'll see. Just come."

My eyes narrowed with suspicion. *Rebirthing? What the hell is this now?*

Chris leaned over to hug me. "It's at the Bank of America building near University Town Center. Bring a pillow and blanket. See you there."

I left without committing.

* * * * *

Back home at my apartment, I paced back and forth, not sure what to do. The skeptical part of me said this was all a bunch of New Age hogwash and I'm probably being scammed. Yet something inside nudged me relentlessly. *Rebirthing? I must be out of my mind!*

I walked into the session with my pillow and blanket, chewing on one lip. The participants, about twenty-five or so, were picking their spots and getting comfortable on their blankets. *This is crazy. What am I doing here?*

Chris greeted me with a warm smile and directed me to a vacant spot. I spread out my blanket on the carpeted floor and sat down.

Chris and the other rebirthers gathered at the front of the room and introduced themselves. Chris, the team leader, began: "I used to be a personnel officer in a large corporation, working nine to five, pushing papers all day long. I made good money, but my soul was dying. Then I discovered rebirthing and saw how it helped people. 'That's what I want to do,' I decided, and let go of the personnel job. Since then, I've seen miracles happen."

Miracles? Hmmm…

The other participants listened with interest.

"Rebirthing is a healing process developed in the 1970s by Leonard Orr," he said, gesturing with his hands. He demonstrated the breathing pattern and we all mimicked him. I noted that this was different from the abdominal yogic breathing I'd learned at the Hindu temple in Tehran.

"The rebirthers will act as your breathing coaches to make sure you keep breathing and don't fall asleep."

How in the world is breathing going to help me with my emotional problems? As if hearing my thoughts, Chris added:

"You may feel stuck emotions wanting to let go. Remember that you are in a safe place. Relax. It's okay to feel. It's okay to cry."

Cry in front of all these people? I don't think so.

"You might be wondering why we call it rebirthing. The early participants of this process experienced memories of their birth, so the name stuck. While this may happen, it is not necessarily the case. Each person's experience will be different."

Chris explained that all the rebirthers were available for private sessions. "Remember," he added, "don't hold back. Let the emotions come out."

Yeah, right. I lay flat on my blanket and propped my head on the pillow as the music started. Closing my eyes, I decided to go along with what I suspected was really just a charade.

Some people began to cry. Others wailed. One thrashed about. I just lay there and breathed, in and out, figuring that the others were being theatrical and nothing of any significance was going to happen to me. We were near the end of the session when I felt a pressure in my chest, like the "Alien" trying to push outwards and pop me open. I ignored it and kept breathing. The pressure intensified. I thrashed and twisted, trying to shove the pain away.

Chris kneeled at my side and spoke to me softly. "Let it go. You don't have to hold on to the pain anymore." He gently placed his hand on my heart. The pain intensified. I writhed and groaned in agony. "I can't!"

Chris stretched out on the blanket beside me and embraced me in his arms, breathing in harmony with me. My gasping breath slowed, deepened, became rhythmic. Moments of severe agony, then a crack, an opening, a tear and it all poured out, the pain, a torrent of tears, an opening, a release. Safe in his arms, I cried and shook and convulsed and sobbed as the emotions poured out of me. When I eventually calmed, Chris unfolded his arms and sat beside me, a broad smile on his face.

Finally, I opened my eyes and stared at the other participants like a newborn seeing the world for the first time. My bodily tension: gone. The pain in my heart: gone. My skin tingled, coming to life. The people in the room looked beautiful, serene, glowing.

After the session, I stepped out of the building into the cool air. The night was still, the sky a myriad of stars. I felt light as air and oddly at peace with myself and the world.

First Contact

I continued individual rebirthing sessions with Chris for two years—most people do only ten sessions. I felt comfortable, safe with Chris. He preferred male partners so, with no sexual tension to distract us, we became very close. He helped me open up to deeper levels of myself and work through all my issues – my mother's leaving, my difficulties adapting to life in Iran, my low sense of self-esteem and many others. In that time, I also attended numerous seminars and workshops on spirituality, healing, meditation and yoga; worked with practitioners of different healing modalities such as hypnosis, Reiki, color therapy and massage; joined groups to study *The Course of Miracles,* a channeled spiritual text, and *The Science of Mind,* the teachings of Ernest Holmes. My passion to know, to learn, to understand was insatiable. I read and read, then read some more. Slowly, gradually, my emotional turmoil calmed and I believed I was finally seeing the light at the end of the tunnel.

One morning, I was mulling over a problem, asking how it could be solved. I was alone, in a quiet space, when I suddenly heard a voice. Not a booming voice from outside of me like Kevin Costner in *Field of Dreams,* but a soft, gentle voice inside my head. It sounded like my own thoughts, but it was different somehow, like a whispering chime offering a clear, win-win solution to my problem.

I recalled hearing that voice on the day of my operation in 1979. I'd put that incident out of my mind, believing it had been a side effect of the morphine. But, if that were true, what was this? I didn't do drugs. I didn't even drink or smoke. Was I losing my marbles? I recalled several movies where people who "heard voices" were put in insane asylums. What was happening to me? My stomach turned in knots.

I raced upstairs and banged on Chris's office door. Wild and disheveled, I stumbled inside, closed the door behind me, and blurted out: "I'm hearing voices!"

Chris asked me to explain. I described the brief incident in detail. "That's nothing to worry about," he said, sitting back in his chair and crossing his legs. His whole face broke into a smile. "You just heard the voice of Spirit. That's all"

That's all? I slumped into the soft leather chair gaping with incredulity.

I had just made contact with God.

Chapter Four: The Spirit Within

We are not human beings having a spiritual experience; we are spiritual beings having a human experience.

–Pierre Teilhard de Chardin

After hearing my inner voice, I walked about in a daze for the next few days, trying to rationalize, to make some kind of sense out of my experience. I understood that there was a spiritual part to the being I called *me,* and this spiritual me, call it spirit or soul or Higher Self, was the authentic me, but I never, in my wildest dreams, imagined that I could actually *talk* with my spirit. Wasn't this the domain of prophets, seers, saints and holy men? Didn't this require years of deep contemplation and living a spiritual life—in a convent, a temple or a cave?

I had learned, through numerous books and workshops, that the real me *was* spirit; that I was an eternal soul connected to all of life, everywhere, including God; that the whole concept of separation was nothing more than an illusion; that, in truth, a part of God resided in each one of us. I had heard this preached at Religious Science churches and self-improvement workshops, I had read about it in several books, listened to the idea on tapes, I had even accepted this premise as true, yet nothing, *nothing* prepared me for the moment of conscious contact.

Of course, it had happened before, but I hadn't recognized it then. Years earlier, just moments before my surgery, I'd heard an angelic voice, had felt embraced with feelings of being loved and protected and cared for. How had that happened? Was it because I truly needed it at that moment? Or was it the morphine, stripping my fears, causing me to let my guard down and drop my defenses? Is it possible that our spirits are there, all the time, like guardian angels, watching over us, guiding us, *talking to us,* but our walls, our mindsets, our beliefs are so thick, so convoluted and confused, that we don't even hear the voice of our own souls?

I now understand why some religions and shamans use psychedelic drugs. Don Juan used psychedelic mushrooms to break Carlos Castaneda of his rigid mindset. That is one route, but it is a shortcut and, in my view, a dangerous one.

I had never taken drugs. I had never meditated or prayed for hours on end, or forsaken the world to dedicate my life to God or spiritual enlightenment. How, then, was it possible for me to hear my spirit after all these years? Thirty-five years on this earth and then—poof! It suddenly shows up? Why? How?

Guided by Spirit – The Inner Voice

My personal experience, in addition to research and inquiry, taught me that our soul or spirit, that still small voice within, contacts and guides us in ways that are acceptable to us based on our cultural orientation and our belief systems. In some instances, it comes as a soft whisper in the night, barely perceptible. It may be just a hunch, a gut feeling, a flash of inspiration, a crystal clear thought or solution to a problem, popping out of nowhere. It could come in the form of an urge, an image, a sensation, a feeling, a phrase or a comment that rings true. It may appear in the form of intuition, a feeling of what to do and what to avoid, or gentle words of encouragement and guidance in response to a prayer or request for help.

Does this guidance come from what Christians call the *Holy Spirit?* Unity church founders Charles and Myrtle Filmore provide the following explanations:

"The Holy Spirit is the activity of God-Mind in the consciousness of men." (*Myrtle Fillmore: Mother of Unity,* T.E. Witherspoon, p. 277)

"Those who look to the Holy Spirit for guidance find that *its* instruction is given to all who believe in Christ, and they are often drawn together by direction of the inner voice, or by a dream, or by a vision." (Charles Filmore, *The Twelve Powers of Man,* p. 75).

Mahatma Gandhi shared his own revelations of the inner voice:

> "For me, The Voice of God, of Conscience, of Truth, or the Inner Voice or 'the Still Small Voice' mean one and the same thing. I saw no form. I have never tried, for I have always believed God to be without form. But what I did hear was like a voice from afar and yet quite near. It was as unmistakable as some human

voice definitely speaking to me, and irresistible. I was not dreaming at the time I heard the Voice. The hearing of the Voice was preceded by a terrific struggle within me. Suddenly the Voice came upon me. I listened, made certain it was The Voice, and the struggle ceased. I was calm. The determination was made accordingly, the date and the hour of the fast were fixed."
(Harijan, 8.7.1933)

In the Jewish mystical tradition called the *Kabbalah,* students yearn for direct connection with the divine, to hear the *Bat Kol,* the still small voice within. Jewish scholar Rav Kook writes:

"The perpetual prayer of the soul continually tries to emerge from its latent state to become revealed and actualized, to permeate every fiber of the entire universe…Sudden spiritual clarity comes about as a result of a certain spiritual lightening bolt that enters the soul…When many days or years have passed without listening to this inner voice, toxic stones gather around one's heart, and one feels, because of them, a certain heaviness of spirit…The primary role of spiritual clarity is for the person to return to himself (herself), to the root of his soul." (Olat Ra'aya, *Introduction to the Prayer book*)

The Sufi Master, Hazrat Inayat Khan, states:

"If only we would recognize the inner voice, we would see that the different scriptures all contain words spoken by one and the same voice.

> Some hear the voice, others only hear the words, just as in nature some see only the branches and others the roots of the tree; but all these scriptures and ways of worship and of contemplating God are given for one purpose: the realization of unity."

The "aha" moment had finally arrived. Ed had functioned as a catalyst, triggering an awakening process that I could not stop—like an avalanche crashing down a mountainside, it had taken on a life of its own. When the pain became so excruciating that I could no longer bear it, I cried out for help. When help arrived in the form of Chris and the new world of spirituality and metaphysics—I made a vow. I would heal myself AND I would spiritually evolve. I would do whatever it took to get there. And so, three long years after reuniting with Ed, after all the healing work, ripping off and discarding layer upon layer of fears, doubts, and outdated beliefs, I had finally created an opening and reached the spirit within me.

The voice of my soul, as for all peoples in every culture and religion, had been there, in the center of my being, all along. *I* had finally begun to listen.

<u>The Ego Battles</u>

I tried to explain these new experiences to my husband, Bahman. He listened, twiddling his mustache, feigning understanding, yet his eyes showed confusion. He had no frame of reference for my "out there in the twilight zone" experiences. He didn't know what to say or how to respond. At the same time, I wrestled with the voices of doubt and fear: *Who do you think you are--Joan of Arc? Why would spirit talk to you? You're delusional.*

A week after making first contact, I awoke to the now-familiar anxiety in my gut. The clock on my dresser said 7:30 a.m. – too early to call Chris. I paced back and forth in my apartment until 8:00, then dialed his number.

"Chris? It's Patti. I need an emergency rebirthing session."

"Not again!" he cried, remembering my early rebirthing days when my body would shake, my stomach knot, and my arms take on a life of their own. We had had a number of "emergency" rebirths in those days to calm me down.

"I'm anxious. My hands are shaking. I can't eat, can't sleep. I've tried everything, but I can't calm down."

"You understand what this is?"

I paused for a second, thinking of what I had learned over the years. "My ego acting up?"

"Good. As long as we're clear here. See you at ten o'clock."

I arrived at his door, panting in desperation. Sweat beaded my forehead. My arms were moving uncontrollably—twitching and shaking.

Chris gave me a warm hug, had me lie on the bed and breathe, deep and slow, suggesting that I become calm and relaxed, reminding me that this was just my ego protesting the fact that I had made contact with my spirit. *Ego* loved to be in charge of my life and didn't want to share this with Spirit. Listening to Chris's deep, soothing voice, the tension in my body dissipated. I drifted in a state of total bliss. Soft music filled the room as Chris began to pray.

I ran to Chris for these "emergency" sessions every so often as my inner war of disbelief raged on. Slowly, over the course of several months, my mind calmed and I began to assimilate the idea that I could communicate with the spiritual part of myself, with my own soul.

I wondered if this is what a "spiritual warrior" is—a person who stands against the avalanche of fears and doubts, goes up against the social norms and belief systems of the time and walks to the beat of a different drum—his or her individual path. I thought of a cartoon I'd seen with a tiny angel sitting on one shoulder and a devil perched on the other. Did these images symbolize the ego and the spirit? Was the war of good and evil not really an outer war, as some religious groups would have us believe, but an inner war between the different parts of our own being? Could this be the real meaning behind the battle of *Ahura Mazda* (God) and *Ahriman* (The Devil) in Zoroastrian beliefs? Did Buddha subdue his own ego to achieve enlightenment under the Bodhi tree? Was Jesus actually challenged by the Christian devil in the desert, or were the temptations simply of his own ego? Could this inner war be the real meaning of *jihad* in Islam?

I had no clear answers to these questions, but a new, different, and much broader picture of spirituality and the spiritual path was forming in my mind.

The path to God is within.

NEW ABILITIES

I was passing a banyan tree in Balboa Park when my palms began to tingle. *This is odd.* I examined my hands. Finding nothing unusual, I shrugged and moved on. As I got farther away from the tree, the tingling in my palms lessoned, then totally disappeared.

I stopped, glanced at my hands, then back at the huge banyan. *No way!* But, like an itch that wouldn't go away, I just had to know. I turned and walked back to the tree, palms facing forward. The banyan's hanging roots looked like legs, as if any minute it could pick up its roots and take a stroll down Fourth Avenue. The palms of my hands began to tingle again, increasing in intensity as I approached the banyan.

Weird!

I experimented by walking all around the park, approaching trees and bushes of various shapes and sizes. The sensations were fainter with a bush, but still there. I tried a dead tree stump—nothing. A telephone pole—nothing. *Can I actually feel the life force of the trees?*

* * * * *

And my experience with the banyan tree was only the beginning. People's emotions and feelings began to affect me in the most profound way. It felt good, no, *wonderful* to be in places where people were happy – on a cruise ship, at an amusement park, or any place where groups of people were in high spirits. I felt lighter, more alive, my energy smooth, flowing. When I participated in groups focused on spiritual activities such as church, meditation, or group rebirths, I glided out of the session high as a kite.

The opposite was also true. Tense situations at work became more than uncomfortable—they became unbearable. Going to malls, especially during the holiday rush with everyone in a frantic mood, made me feel drained and bone tired, like a vampire had sucked out every ounce of my blood. Dealing with angry people became impossible, as if my energy field reacted to theirs and became jagged, irregular. I could *sense* the other person's charged emotions as if they were my own.

The most bizarre experiences came when I interacted with two-faced people. It was like watching a cartoon in which a character says one thing, but a little bubble above his head says the opposite. I felt queasy just talking to these people, so I'd try to make my interactions as brief as possible and only when necessary.

On rare occasions, I had premonitions. The information would come as a soft whisper in my mind, an image flashing across my consciousness, or just a feeling—and events happened just as I knew they would. Much to my chagrin, this ability did not show up on demand; instead, it popped up randomly.

By talking to others and reading about people who had had similar experiences, I learned that these so-called psychic or sixth-sense abilities are nothing unusual. Everybody has them, but most people block them out. This realization did not make the experiences any less disconcerting, but at least it gave me some degree of comfort to know that I was not alone.

The Light Spot

An early morning dream:

I have no body, no form. I see others like me, lining up. I understand that they are volunteering for a mission of great importance and high honors. I get in line.

We break up into groups and discuss meeting and working with one another at specific time and places during the mission. I eagerly attend these planning sessions and proudly agree to do whatever it takes to succeed.

While on the mission, it's imperative that a specific frequency remain open at all times. Further instructions will be given as needed. I am warned that this culture is alluring; that it has seduced some of the mission's best agents. I emphasize my commitment and set off to my assigned destination, disguised as one of the locals.

Years pass.

The exotic culture has seduced me into a drunken stupor. I have disguised myself so well that I believe this is who I really am. I have altered my behavior to match the locals and have forgotten that there once was another way of thinking or being. I have tuned out the frequency and no longer hear the instructions given me. I have no recollection of my original purpose.

But now, finally, at age thirty-five, I am remembering. I understand my original purpose; I remember my assignment data:

Destination: Earth
Disguise: Human
Mission: Remember who you are and fulfill the purpose of your soul.

* * * * *

I woke up with a jerk in my San Diego apartment. Images poured into my mind, fast and furious. My eyes flew open. *A bookstore! Yes!*

I grabbed a yellow pad and wrote furiously, my hand cramping as I tried to keep up with the avalanche of information. The bright California sun poured through cracks in the curtain and spread across the bed. Bahman poked his head from under the covers and raised a quizzical eyebrow. I ignored him and kept writing. The dream had been so vivid, so real. I had come here for a purpose. I had actually *volunteered* to come here, to be born as a human being. And the next step in my life's path was being shown to me--a bookstore and coffeehouse, a cozy little place painted in light colors. I was working there, behind the counter, greeting people.

Intoxicated with this information, I explained my new calling to Bahman. He gazed at me through sleepy eyes.

I called Ed in San Francisco.

"Guess what," I said, twirling the telephone cord with one finger.

"Hi, munchkin. What are you up to now?"

"I'm going to open a business."

A moment of silence.

"Um, what kind of business?"

"A bookstore and coffeehouse. I saw it all in a vision. I'm calling it The Light Spot.

"Do you know how to run a business?" His words were slow, almost patronizing.

"No, but this is something I just know I'm going to do—have to do."

"Ah… where are you going to get the money?"

"I have the money I saved up for the down payment on a house. Bahman doesn't seem to like any house we look at anyway. We've given up searching."

"Well, good luck with it." He didn't sound convinced. He probably thought it was just a pipe dream.

I explained everything to Chris that afternoon, wild with excitement. Chris nodded. "I've been thinking about getting an office, too—someplace outside of my home where I can meet my rebirthing clients." He tapped one finger on his cheek, deep in thought.

"Maybe we'll be close to each other," I said, a big smile on my face. I liked the prospect of spending more time with Chris. He had become much more than my practitioner and rebirther. He had become my best friend.

"Why don't we treat?" He leaned forward, picked up my hands, and we did a Spiritual Mind Treatment for The Light Spot's location.

Chapter Five: The Power of Creation

We are what we think. All that we are arises with our thoughts. With our thoughts, we make the world.

–Buddha

A few weeks after our Spiritual Mind Treatment, the location for The Light Spot presented itself via one of Chris's clients—a building in Hillcrest, near downtown San Diego with available retail space downstairs, parking out front, plus two offices and a meeting room on the second floor.

The space on the lower level faced Fifth Avenue with high traffic and good visibility. Nevertheless, finding the location was only the first step. I still had to work with property managers, carpenters, painters, booksellers, music merchants, plumbers, coffee-machine leasers, carpet people, government licensing agents, health inspectors, crystals sales people, coffee and confection wholesalers, and God knows how many others.

Things did not always go smoothly: the carpenter disappeared half way through the job, the plumber used the wrong kind of pipes and the job had to be redone, the property manager refused to put in a hot water heater unless I paid for it, the carpet layer used the wrong padding, the health inspector didn't like the flooring and the vents—he said cockroaches could get in—and the new restaurant next door complained that I would be taking away their business by selling coffee and pastries.

I didn't have the foggiest idea which books and tapes to order or what people would want to buy, and on top of it all, I still had to hold on to my teaching job to make a living. In spite of it all, in the spring of 1985, I proudly opened The Light Spot Bookstore and Coffeehouse, offering crystals for healing, books on self-help and metaphysics, and tapes for relaxation, inspiration, and meditation. The shop was decorated in soothing colors—light grays, soft pinks and natural wood—and filled with the heady scent of incense and the aroma of freshly brewed coffee.

Chris and I became partners in the upstairs area, which we called The Inner Visions Center. He took one office where he met with clients for rebirthing and Science of Mind practitioner work. A chiropractor and a massage therapist shared the second office. The large meeting room became a central location for a variety of activities and classes in spiritual development and personal growth.

Chris was the charismatic front person who attracted people to our little center with his bubbly personality and people skills. I took care of all the details. Following my vision, I now had a purpose, a calling. Life was rich and full.

Thoughts and Form

I had learned through Terry Cole-Whittaker, Chris, and the teachings of Ernest Holmes about the power of creation, the ability to make changes in your life through your words and thoughts. And while I like to keep an open mind about such things, I also tend to maintain a healthy dose of skepticism. How could mere *thoughts* change reality? This didn't make sense. Changing your reality took *planning, work, effort* and perseverance, no matter what. True, the location for The Light Spot had shown up with little effort on my part, but this could have been pure coincidence. And the location had been only the first step in a long, arduous process.

So, where did "thought" come into all of this? Where did the creative power of Spirit show up to make things work?

I discovered numerous methods and techniques to help focus my mind in order to manifest my reality. Never one to take anything at face value, I just had to try them out and see what happened.

Methods for Creating Your Own Reality

Spiritual Mind Treatment—Praying with another person using the technique suggested by Ernest Holmes. Both individuals align in mind for the desired outcome.

Meditation--relaxing mind and body and either requesting or holding the picture of your desired outcome in mind.

Affirmations--writing or repeating the desired outcome over and over again.

Visualization—creating the image of your desired outcome in mind with as much detail and sensory input as possible and focusing on it.

Ritual—focusing the mind using candles, incense, drums, chimes, and other paraphernalia, then declaring your desire out loud.

Hypnosis—training the unconscious mind to accept a new idea with the help of a qualified hypnotist, then creating a symbol to represent it. This symbol is posted in different places in your environment in order to focus and reinforce the new concept.

Treasure Maps—cutting out and pasting pictures, images, and words of your wants and desires on a cardboard poster or a photo album and placing it in a location where you can view it regularly.

Subliminals—listening to taped music recordings with subliminal messages of your desired outcome.

Mastermind™—meeting with a group of individuals every week, stating your wants and desires, and allowing the group to affirm that you can have that in your life and vice versa.

I realized that all of these so-called "methods," were actually doing the same thing – focusing the mind. By trial and error, I learned that scattered thoughts rarely produce results. Creating or "manifesting" requires focus, attention, and trust. In my experience, some creations came about quickly, while others had a much longer lag time.

A Clean Car

I loved my snow-white Honda Civic. Chris had talked me into buying it since my Escort just didn't have enough *zip*. "You're not an old lady," he said. "Why drive a car that acts like one?"

The Honda, with its lighter body, picked up speed on the highway in a matter of seconds. I named it *Pee-Wee*, pampered it like a baby, and kept it spotless. But nowadays I was living life full boogey: teaching my ESL courses, running The Light Spot, managing The Inner Visions Center, booking Chris's clients, and participating in numerous metaphysical classes and workshops. With such a full plate, cleaning the car did not take top priority.

One morning, I parked behind The Light Spot and was getting out of the car when I noticed how dirty the car's floors had become. I crinkled my nose in disgust and scanned the exterior, too. *My poor little Pee-Wee. She's filthy and I don't have the time to take care of her. . I wish I could find someone who would get the job done for a reasonable price.*

About an hour later, a man carrying a bucket, sponge, rags, liquid soap and window cleaner stepped into my store.

"Clean your car inside and out for just $25, ma'am," he said, dark eyes gleaming.

My mouth hung open as I stared at him in disbelief.

My car sparkled as I drove it home that day.

The Treasure Map

In 1987, I was taking a class from the minister at the Church of Religious Science. The primary focus of this class was taking personal responsibility for our lives. "In order to change your life, you first have to change your thoughts and focus on your desired outcome," the minister said. She then assigned us homework: "Create a Treasure Map in a photo album using pictures, images, words and phrases that portray your ideal life."

I slumped on the couch in a classmate's apartment, paging through a fashion magazine. Others were cutting out pictures or searching among the piles of different publications strewn across the floor. Some of my classmates were looking for images of specific things: love, money, a car, a house, a great body... *What do I want my future to look like?* I had never thought about it much. I'd just floated through life, willy nilly, letting come what may. I had lived mostly in the *now*, and although I had heard that this was a good thing, I knew that if I desired to manifest my ideal future, I would have to focus on what I wanted.

I flipped through a number of magazines, scanning page after page of colorful people, places, and material things. *What do I really want?* I grabbed a travel magazine and came across a picture of a cruise ship. *It would be nice to go on a cruise some day,* I thought as I cut out the picture and pasted it into my album. At the time, I had no sense of a specific destination, but just wanted the experience of a cruise.

Many years later, long after I'd forgotten all about the class, I was lounging on the deck of a cruise ship sailing to the Bahamas. Waiters offered tall, cool drinks topped with colorful umbrellas and adorned with sun glasses. I leaned back in a lounge chair, breathing in the clear ocean air. Suddenly the image of that cruise ship picture I had cut out years earlier popped into my head. *I wonder where that ship was heading?*

The thought lingered in the back of my mind all through the vacation. When I returned home, I just had to know. I rummaged through closets, through drawers, through the garage, through the attic—through bags, through piles, through box after box, and then, when I was just about ready to give up on the whole thing, there it was, at the bottom of a dusty box, long forgotten.

I picked up the album, its orange cover faded and cracked, and hugged it to my chest—my very first treasure map. I've made numerous others since that time, most of them on poster board so I could hang them on the wall and see them on a daily basis. Flipping though the pages, I found the photo of the cruise ship and paused, staring at the picture, trying to wrap my head around the truth of it all.

The picture showed a ship sailing on a deep blue sea, with a map of the Bahamas in the distance.

Our World Mirrors Our Beliefs

Through my many classes, workshops, and readings, I've learned that we are all fields of energy vibrating at different frequencies or, as Carlos Castaneda explained it, "luminous spheres of energy." Our thoughts, our emotions, and our belief systems affect the frequency of our energetic fields which then function like magnets attracting or repelling people and experiences into our lives. In other words, our world is a mirror of our innermost feelings and beliefs. When we change our beliefs, we can change our world.

These ideas were influenced by many spiritual and esoteric teachers in the late nineteenth century such as Madame Blavatsky (Theosophy), Rudolph Steiner (Anthroposophy), and Carl Jung (Archetypal Psychology), in addition to Dr. Ernest Holmes (Science of Mind). The Church of Religious Science, based on Holmes' teachings, made popular the concept of changing reality by the power of thought.

While Holmes was influential in spreading the idea that your thoughts influence your world, the concept is anything but new and has been practiced by various peoples throughout the ages. Consider the following concepts:

- *Magic* is the art and science of using the will to change reality. The Druids of Ireland used magic to help their tribes win wars.

- *Alchemy,* in its truest sense, is a means of altering patterns within our own energy fields. In other words, transmuting *leaden* thoughts and patterns that create suffering in our lives into *gold* thoughts and patterns which bring happiness and fulfillment.

- *Healing* has been used by shamans the world over to help rid a patient of disease and illness through ceremony, ritual, and aligning with Spirit.

- *The Breath*, or *ha,* the Hawai'ian *kupunas* say, carries your words and manifests your reality.

- *The Word,* as stated in the Bible, is what God used to create the world. Since we are all God-sparks disguised as humans, we also use the power of the Word to create. Author and teacher Don Muguel Ruiz, in his book, *The Four Agreements,* says: "Be impeccable with your word." Why? Because we all use the power of our words to create. Our words carry our intent, our beliefs, and our feelings. Our words create our world, our reality--beautiful or horrific, it's our choice.

<u>Why Doesn't It Work?</u>

The Light Spot was a magical place that introduced me to an array of new and wonderful people and ideas. Every day, my concepts and beliefs about reality and the world were challenged, my mind stretched. I was changing and transforming at an accelerated rate, scrambling to keep up and digest it all. I had followed my inner guidance to create The Light Spot, a place that provided the appropriate environment for my own evolution and growth in consciousness. I had built it, but, unlike the ball field in the movie *Field of Dreams,* the customers didn't come. Not enough of them, anyway, to make a profit, much less a living. The Light Spot was in financial trouble.

I rebirthed to let go of any belief systems of lack and limitation that might be blocking my success. I did Spiritual Mind Treatments with Chris. I meditated; I visualized; I made treasure maps; I wrote affirmations until I was blue in the face. The Light Spot survived another day, another week, another month, but barely. Always hanging on by a thread, I constantly worried whether I would be able to make payroll or cover the rent.

"It's just not happening!" I complained to Chris, biting off a piece of chocolate chip cookie. "I've tried everything. It's not working."

"Worrying won't help matters," Chris replied, pouring himself a cup of coffee and pulling up a chair. "Your mind is in the wrong place. Focus on what you want, not what you don't want."

I hated to admit it, but he was right. "So why is the time lag so different? Why do some things happen quickly while others take months or even years? What's the difference?"

Chris put down his coffee cup and grinned. "It has to do with your beliefs. If you believe that something is possible, then it happens quickly. If you don't believe it, if you have fears or judgments about it, you'll have to work on making the inner changes before anything can happen on the outside."

I had no beliefs against someone showing up to clean my car, and so it had happened quickly. But a cruise? I'd always thought that was something rich people did. Convincing myself that I deserved to do the same, that I was "worthy" of such an extravagance, took several years. Hmmm…

Chris went upstairs to meet a client. I sat behind the counter, pondering this process of manifestation. *Maybe the whole thing wasn't about manifesting at all. Maybe this was the way things were set up in order to nudge us into facing our fears, our judgments, and our outdated beliefs. Could it be that the whole game is about the inner healing and transformation and that the goal or object of our desire is just the carrot?*

Still concerned about The Light Spot, I went to see a prominent psychic.

"Why am I not making any money?" I asked, sitting across from her.

"Making money was never your intention," she replied, matter-of-factly.

"Huh?" I stared at her dumbfounded. "But it's a business!"

"True." She leaned forward, looking at me with intense blue eyes. "But your real intention when creating it was *not* to make money."

I thought back and had to admit she was right. When I created The Light Spot, making money was not even on my mind. My focus, my *intent,* was to follow my inner guidance, spend more time with Chris, learn new things, meet new people, and have new experiences, all of which I had accomplished. Making money had never even been a consideration.

LETTING GO OF FEAR

Chris was studying at a school in Escondido, California to become a hypnotist. As part of the curriculum, the instructor planned a fire walk for his students. Friends and relatives could also participate for a nominal fee.

It's next Saturday," Chris said, charming me with his broad smile. "Will you join me?"

I stopped my coffee mug midair and gawked at him from across the table. "You mean walk across hot coals?"

"Yes, but he'll have us hypnotized, so you won't even realize that you're walking on fire."

"I don't know," I said, getting up to help a customer who wanted to purchase a book. I poured another cup of coffee and rejoined Chris.

"One of my clients, Sharon, is also coming. It'll be fun."

"Walking across hot coals and getting your feet burned is not my definition of fun," I replied, slurping my coffee to avoid his gaze. I wondered if he just wanted my company or if he wanted me there because he was afraid himself. Probably both.

"It will help you face your deepest fears. What are your fears right now?"

A young woman in faded jeans stepped into the shop and began examining the crystals. I put the cup down and looked up at Chris. "Losing the Light Spot."

He leaned back in his chair and crossed his legs, a triumphant look on his face. "If you hold on to that fear, you'll manifest it. It's time to face it and let it go."

Chris won. I agreed to go.

* * * * *

It was a cool, summer evening. We sat in a large classroom, about fifty of us, eyes darting this way and that, none quite sure of ourselves, many looking for an excuse to bolt. The instructor, a husky man with raven hair and a goatee, gave us a brief introduction about the process, then directed us to write down all our fears related to the fire walk. I wrote furiously, my hand trembling as I realized all the possible things that could go wrong, such as burning the soles of my feet. After we were done, we paired up and shared our fears with one another. Beads of sweat formed on my forehead and dripped down my face, even though it was cool in the room.

A man poked his head in the door and announced that the fire had been lit. The instructor guided us down the stairs and out into the yard. Flames, several feet high, licked the pile of wood and danced in the early evening air. My face grew warm, then hot by the intensity of the fire. One by one, we advanced and tossed our notes into the fire, watching our fears burst into flames and burn to ashes. I flipped my list of fears in the fire, feeling a sense of release as it burned, the ashes floating up into the night sky.

Returning to the classroom, we watched videos of fire walks in different cultures. Seeing other people walk across fire with no ill effects was encouraging, but did not calm my knotted stomach.

After a short break, the instructor informed us that the woodpile was ready to receive us. I glanced at Chris with trepidation, feeling like I wanted to puke. He grimaced and stood up. We clasped hands and trailed the others down the steps and out into the yard under the starry sky. The wood had burned down to coals and had been raked into a walkway about four feet wide and fifteen feet long. Red glowing embers were visible beneath a layer of ash. The instructor crumpled a paper and tossed it onto the coals. We all gasped as it burst into flames.

I glanced at Chris. His face was contorted in a grimace, beads of sweat drizzling down his face. *Why in the world did I let him talk me into this? It's insane!*

With wide eyes and pounding hearts, we lingered around the walkway of burning coals. The instructor chanted: "Cool, soft snow."

We joined in, slowly at first. "Cool, soft snow. Cool, soft snow."

Our voices gathered momentum and filled the evening sky. Some clapped in beat with the chant. People began to sway, eyes glazing over as if in a trance. A tingling sensation ran up my arms and down my spine. I continued to chant as loudly as I could as if this would allay my fears. "Cool, soft snow. Cool, soft snow."

The instructor removed his socks and shoes, rolled up his pants, and stepped onto the coals. The crowd chanted, "Cool, soft snow," clapping and swaying to the rhythm.

The instructor advanced across the coals in his bare feet, slowly, meticulously. We all watched, wide-eyed, chanting, swaying. He reached the end of the walkway of fire and stepped off the coals onto the cool grass. A few students scuttled over to check his feet.

"Cool, soft snow. Cool, soft snow." The chanting continued, a jumble of fears, anxieties, anticipation and wonder filling the night. The instructor waited patiently. Our voices joined together, rose, reached a crescendo.

Heads turned as one brave soul stepped forward. We all stood, transfixed. "Cool, soft snow."

After him, a few others began to line up.

I moved to the end of the burning walkway and carefully checked the feet of those who had walked across. No burns. *If they can do it, I can do it.* I took off my shoes and rolled up my pants. Shoulders squared, chin jutted out, I stepped to the front of the walkway of fire.

The instructor tapped my shoulder. "Your turn." I swallowed and stepped onto the coals.

"Cool, soft snow. Cool, soft snow," the chanting swirled around me like a protective cloak. The embers crunched under my feet. I imagined walking on snow, cool and soft and safe. To my amazement, I experienced no sensation of heat on the soles of my feet.

I reached the end and stepped onto the grass. Chris glanced at me, then walked across himself. A few feet from the walkway, he found me sitting on the ground, staring at the bottom of my blackened, but unharmed feet. I was having a hard time digesting this. I looked up at Chris. "I'm going again."

"Let's go together," he said. We stepped up to the front of the walkway, arms locked, and marched across triumphantly.

That night, I sat in the bathtub, examining the soles of my feet. It was one of the strangest feelings I could ever remember. My logical mind would not accept this. Fire burns. I walked on fire barefoot, but didn't burn. How? This did not happen. This could not have happened. It did not make logical sense. I felt like the robot in *Lost in Space,* waving its arms wildly: "Does not compute! Does not compute!"

Finally, I searched between my toes and discovered a tiny burn on the inner part of my small toe, barely perceptible. A small piece of coal had lodged itself between my toes and remained there for a brief moment after I had completed the fire walk. I lay back in the tub and took a deep breath. *I really did it!*

My mind expanded like a child's balloon. Sinking into the warm water, I smiled to myself. I knew that from now on *fear* would no longer hold me back; that I'd have the Light Spot bookstore and coffeehouse as long as it needed to be a part of my life.

Chapter Six: Making a Difference

The world is full of mediocre people. Do you want to be one of them?

—Terry Cole-Whittaker

A colorful array of patrons frequented The Light Spot Bookstore and Coffeehouse. We had the curious ones, who didn't know where to start. "Begin here," I'd say, handing them *Love is Letting Go of Fear* by Gerald Jampolsky. Then, there were those in the know, who'd ask me, "Have you read so and so's latest book? It's life changing. Will you be ordering it for the store?" Others, casual passersby, dropped in for a cup of coffee while eyeing the tapes, the crystals, the book titles, and the quotes from *A Course in Miracles* on the walls.

We were visited by gentle monks in orange robes, tough women in leather motorcycle jackets, clean-cut professional men in suits, hippies with long, unkempt hair; environmentalists who suggested I use biodegradable coffee cups, a Hare Krishna with his drum, a Sikh in his turban, and a Wiccan proudly displaying her pentagon necklace.

Some female customers dressed in crisp business attire, while others wore long earrings and flowing skirts or casual jeans and T's.

Our regulars included a young man named Paul who read tarot cards for customers and introduced me to pagan spirituality; a tall German and his girlfriend who taught me Reiki (healing with one's hands); a chiropractor who rented an office upstairs; a yoga teacher who held weekly classes; and two elderly gay men who enjoyed late afternoon espresso coffee out on the deck, made just so.

Some spent hours in the back room looking through the many books and sipping herbal tea. Others came in search of healing crystals, soothing music, or videos like Richard's Bach's *Jonathon Livingston Seagull,* a presentation on love from Leo Buscalgio, a chakra meditation by Shirley Maclain, the spiritual quest of Gurdjieff in *Meetings with Remarkable Men,* or a talk on compassion by the Dalai Lama.

A mild-mannered Columbian man, a previous student of mine, minded the shop while I taught my ESL classes for the local college or managed the center. Our monthly newsletter included a calendar of center events, book reviews, and personal insights and experiences. People enjoyed receiving them and my mailing list grew. And while The Light Spot still didn't make much money, it wasn't a major concern. My life had taken on new colors, textures, and flavors. I no longer just existed; I was living and contributing and it felt good.

THE HOMELESS MAN

Homeless people dropped by The Light Spot every now and then. I usually offered them coffee and pastries, but no money, believing they would use it to purchase alcohol or drugs.

One evening, about half an hour before closing, a homeless man stepped into the shop.

"May I have a cup of coffee?" Sad green eyes peered out at me through an unshaven, grubby face framed by a mass of disheveled hair. He was dressed in several layers of mismatched clothes with scuffed shoes that barely held together. No reek of alcohol. No glazed eyes or enlarged pupils. He was neither drunk nor on drugs.

"No problem." I smiled, reaching for a paper cup so he could have it to go. As I lifted the coffee pot to pour, however, the man pulled out a chair and sat down at a table.

I shrugged, and poured the coffee into a ceramic mug instead, serving it along with a plate of blueberry muffins and oatmeal cookies.

"Thank you." He nodded.

I smiled and turned to step back behind the counter.

"Will you join me?"

I froze in midstep. *Every person is a God-being disguised as a human. As they say, "walk your talk."*

"No problem." I attempted to sound calm and collected. I didn't really want to sit with this dirty, disheveled man. Nevertheless, I poured myself a cup of coffee, placed a blueberry muffin on a plate, and, ignoring my discomfort, pulled up a chair.

He wrapped his grimy hands around the warm cup and sipped. Several moments passed in silence. I broke my muffin into pieces and began to munch.

"I wasn't always a homeless person," he said, pain evident in his eyes. He fished out a worn leather wallet and placed it on the table between us, pulling out several cards and photos. "I used to be a pilot. An airline pilot. See, here is my license."

An airline pilot? How could an airline pilot turn into a homeless man? I stared as he laid the cards and photos on the round wooden table.

The pilot's license displayed a picture of the man: younger, clean shaven, but definitely him. I sensed a chill, like a cold wind had suddenly blown in. I had assumed that people became homeless due to their own weak wills or lack of effort, that they were drunks or drug addicts or lazy people who refused to work for a living. I thought they were people to be feared. I had summarily judged and condemned and dismissed them without background information, without evidence, without foundation, without even conscious thought. I had never imagined that an educated professional could meet such a fate. My stomach churned. I opened my eyes and got a good look at the darker side of myself. I didn't like what I saw.

The homeless man displayed other cards, proof of organizations he had belonged to, of the airline he had worked for, of things he had accomplished. I examined each card with wide eyes, wondering why he had chosen this night to share his life; wondering if he realized the profound effect this was having on me. He had shattered my beliefs about homeless people, breaking them into tiny pieces scattered about the room. *What other misguided assumptions and judgments do I hold about people?*

He finally dug deep into his wallet and reverently pulled out one last photograph and laid it on the table, his hand shaking.

"My wife and daughter." The last word caught in his throat.

I examined the photo: it was old, cracked. He was young and clean cut, his wife fair with shoulder-length hair, his daughter about five or six with bright blue eyes.

"What happened to them?"

His eyes swelled with tears. "They were in a plane crash."

He gave no further explanation. The silence stretched. Outside, two men strolled past the shop, chatting merrily about a show. A car horn beeped on the street.

"They were beautiful," I said, handing him back the photograph with the same reverence that he had displayed. I rose to get a box of Kleenex.

An hour past closing, we were still sitting at the round wooden table covered with cookie crumbs and empty coffee cups. Leaning forward, he engulfed my small hands within his large, dirty ones and looked me straight in the eye. "You're a kind woman. God bless you."

He rose to leave. I collected the cups and saucers and carried them behind the counter. With a brief nod of his head he slipped out the door.

* * * * *

I grappled with the ripples of that night for some time. My encounter with the homeless man had shaken me deeply, loosening buried belief systems that I could no longer hold on to if I were to progress on my spiritual path. This man had, beyond doubt, been the one to teach me that night; he showed me that I should never make assumptions about the lives of others, their sacred contracts and their purpose. He also caused me to vividly see that the teachings of Spirit can come anytime, anywhere, from anyone. The key is to pay attention.

I pondered the homeless man's situation. Why would the soul of this man choose such a difficult life? Was this a random happening due to life circumstances, or was it something the soul had actually *agreed* to as part of its reason and purpose for being here? Could it be that its particular lesson, the growth the soul was seeking, *required* such great sacrifice?

Could it be that some souls incarnated in difficult life circumstances in order to function as catalysts for others? In order to create *opportunities* for other souls to feel, to give, to open, to gain a greater understanding of who they are? If this premise is true, was it possible that the helpers, the caretakers, the good Samaritans and philanthropists of the world are the ones *receiving* the lessons from the very people they are helping?

The Gifts We Bring

Rays of the early morning sun spread across the hardwood floor of The Light Spot like fingers attempting to reach the opposite wall. The aroma of freshly-brewed coffee filled the shop. I leaned back in the wooden chair and stretched my legs to catch the warm rays while pondering the visit of the homeless man a few days before. *If life has meaning and purpose, then it stands to reason that each and every one of us has a unique gift to give to the world—a contribution that will serve a higher cause.* Wrapping my fingers around my coffee mug, I gazed out the door. My rainbow-colored umbrellas, shading the white metal tables and chairs on the deck, flapped in the morning breeze. Traffic was already dense as people hustled every which way. *Some people probably spend a lifetime in preparing for the gift they will give. Others may offer their gifts in small increments. Nevertheless, we all add to the richness of the human family; we all affect the world, regardless of appearances.*

I sipped my café latte. The shop was brighter now—the crystals sparkled in their case, beckoning customers to purchase them for their powers to balance and heal. The soft pink of the wall played off the turquoise quote from *The Course in Miracles:* "Miracles are natural; when they do not occur, something has gone wrong."

I scanned the shelves filled with books on diverse religions and traditions, many of them claiming to be the one true way.

How can we assume that everyone should go to church on Sundays, or face Mecca to pray, or sit in a temple in contemplative meditation? I mused, lighting an incense stick. Its smoke rose and danced with the dust particles lit up by the sun. The shop became heady with the musky scent. *How can we dictate a prescribed set of practices and beliefs and insist that everyone follow them in order to achieve spiritual enlightenment or ascend to heaven or get off the wheel of karma or whatever the case may be? It's like saying that everyone on earth should like and eat bananas or that everyone should wear the color blue. How can we accept the erroneous belief that one's personal relationship with God can be prescribed by another, as if there were a "one size fits all" spiritual path? Is man trying to create God in his own image rather than the other way around?*

A man in a three-piece suit stepped into the store, his eyes darting about nervously. I sensed his energy shrink when he noticed the crystals and book titles. He requested a cup of coffee, dropped a couple of dollars on the counter, and made a hasty retreat.

So many of us are afraid of the unknown, I mused, watching the man take long strides down the street. *Fear—the primary reason many people prefer to be "told" what to believe, rather than seek answers for themselves and pursue a direct experience of divinity.*

I popped a tape into the stereo and sensed my energy shift, lighten, as the haunting music of Constance Demby filled the room. *Maybe--just as we are each unique in our physical appearance, our fingerprints, and our DNA; just as we have particular ways of expressing our individuality through our lifestyles, the clothes we wear, the food we eat, and the work we do; just as our expressions of love and our relationships take on their own flavor and form—our relationship with God evolves, not out of following the guidelines of dogma or a spiritual leader, but by following the beat of our own drums and making a connection to the divinity within our hearts.*

I smiled to myself. *People create their own ideas of God, then package him neatly in a box and market him like jelly or the latest techno gadget. But this is only their particular interpretation of divinity; one that makes them comfortable and secure. In truth, God is beyond any description we can give him (or her, or it) with our limited human minds.*

God is outside the box.

THE SHAMAN

Shortly after I opened shop on a bright Saturday morning, an enormous figure filled the doorway to The Light Spot—

a barrel-chested man in faded blue jeans and scuffed cowboy boots with thick, raven hair hanging down to his shoulders. An elaborate gold and turquoise necklace adorned his neck and chest, and a leather medicine pouch hung from his beaded belt. "Michael Big Bear," he said, extending his hand.

"Patti Panahi." I shook his hand, rather surprised. Customers did not normally introduce themselves, at least not right away.

"I'd really enjoy a cup of good brew." His eyes were dark as scarabs.

He took a seat to one side of the shop, eyeing the books on the shelves as he sipped the steaming coffee.

"This your place?"

"Yep. Built it from scratch."

He scanned the tapes, the videos, the crystals, the greeting cards. "Have you read many of these books?" He gestured with a sweep of his hand.

"I'm working on it," I replied, displaying the book I was reading, *Creative Visualization* by Shakti Gawain.

He nodded slowly. "I'm a shaman of my tribe. Do you know much about the native ways?"

"No, I don't, actually." I set my book aside. He had my attention.

And so Michael Big Bear began his stories, fantastic tales of shamanic journeys and sand paintings, sweat lodges and healing herbs, experiences he had had, things he had learned, how he had grown to become a powerful medicine man.

Captivated by the shaman's stories like a child hearing her first fairy tales, I took no notice of the passing of time. When the grumbling of our stomachs got our attention, we ordered lunch from the café next door and whiled away the afternoon. He told me how he had helped make peace among Indian shamans, how he had created rain during a serious drought in the Southwest, how he had made predictions with high levels of accuracy, how he had healed several people of serious diseases.

The sun began to set and the sky was a tapestry of orange and rose. Michael Big Bear was quiet now, washing down a cookie with the last bit of coffee in his mug. Setting it on the table, he rose to leave, but lingered near the door, as if something had been left undone.

I watched the imposing shaman from behind the counter, sensing his hesitation.

Look closely, said my inner voice with a gentle nudge. I focused on Michael Big Bear. My vision shifted, as if I were looking through a misty window. I saw a shadow, like a cloud, dark and gray, hovering around his heart area. I didn't think. I didn't rationalize. In a trance-like state, I stepped out from behind the counter, approached the huge man, and placed my open palm on his heart.

"The pain in your heart needs healing," I looked up at him.

He gaped at me in stunned silence, eyes haunted by inner pain. The moment stretched. Those scarab eyes misted over. "My greatest fear is loving." His voice quavered.

He slumped into a chair. I served him another cup of coffee.

"I've done wrong." Tears streaked his face. "I've hurt people. People I loved."

I quietly placed a box of Kleenex on the table and took a chair across from him.

"I'm not proud of what I've done," he said, his face twisted in anguish. "The pain's right here. And it hurts like hell." He thumped his heart with a fist.

I listened quietly, overwhelmed by this strange turn of events.

He wept softly as he spoke, and confessed that he had harmed those he'd loved the most, done things he was not proud of, things he needed to amend.

He gave no details and no further explanation. I didn't feel it prudent to pry, so I just sat with him, listening. I guessed that he was probably talking about a woman, a girlfriend or wife, possibly a child. Words were said that he now regretted. He had abandoned them and locked the pain in his heart – until now.

It was almost dark. He was calm now, his face serene. He rifled through his medicine bag, pulled out several pieces of turquoise, and placed them gently in the palms of my hands—gifts from his native land. I accepted graciously.

We both stood up, his large frame towering over me. He laid his elaborate gold and turquoise necklace around my neck and enveloped me in a bear hug. A jolt of energy shot through my body.

"My life has become enriched and blessed by the time I have spent with you," he said, gently removing the necklace. He looked deep into my eyes for a moment, kissed me softly on the cheek, and disappeared into the night.

All the power and knowledge in the universe is useless if we do not open our hearts and allow ourselves to love. These thoughts came out of nowhere, as if by divine revelation.

Love is the true power of God.

* * * * *

I rarely ever see the human aura. Why was it so visible to me on that day? What possessed me to place my hand on his chest and tell this learned man that he needed to heal his heart, an action completely out of character for me? Was the unseen hand of Spirit guiding me to assist the shaman? Was it because this is what he needed at that time? Do we all become tools of Spirit when the need arises? Was the shaman's visit also a catalyst to help me open my inner vision? The more I learn, the more the world of Spirit remains a mystery.

I owned and operated The Light Spot for about four and a half years, a period of my life when I was flooded with new ideas, mind-boggled with extraordinary experiences, and amazed by the cornucopia of characters that frequented my little corner of the world. But looking at it from a worldly perspective, The Light Spot never made much money, although it survived long enough to facilitate the lessons I needed to learn. My physical needs, fortunately, were provided for by my teaching job and my husband's business.

Was this lack of financial success due to my own belief that it was inappropriate to make a profit by helping people on their spiritual path? The belief that "spiritual work" should be separated from "making money," the realm of the mundane; that there is something "wrong" about making money? Could this deeply embedded belief also be the reason that many in service of Spirit are not financially successful in the world? If I had been able to transform this belief, would the business have been successful?

On the other hand, it might have been very difficult for me to abandon a prospering business when the time came to move on. Would I have hesitated? Resisted the next step? Stayed in San Diego?

While I'll never know the answers to these questions, I have no doubt that opening and managing The Light Spot was a major catalyst in the growth of my soul and I have never regretted it.

Chapter Seven: The Awakening Heart

When we cease thinking primarily about ourselves and our own self-preservation, we undergo a truly heroic transformation of consciousness.

– Joseph Campbell,
The Power of Myth

SAN DIEGO, CALIFORNIA – 1987

We gathered around a rickety wooden table in a local coffee shop, three members of Chris's rebirthing class: Sharon, a no-nonsense, don't-mess-with-me kind of gal who had no qualms about telling you the way it is, her shoulder-length wheat hair spilling forward as she scanned the menu; Dillon, a clean-cut, Midwestern type, his face pale and scrunched, staring vacantly into the streams of customers. And me, thirty-six with short, light brown hair and a few extra pounds padding my hips.

Chris placed steaming café mochas and lattes in front of us and sat across from me. Sharon blew on her coffee before taking a sip. I occupied myself folding paper napkins into tiny triangles. Awkward moments passed. None of us knew what to say that didn't sound stupid or trite. Dillon had been diagnosed with AIDS.

"Have you told your family?" Chris blurted out, breaking that terrible silence.

Sharon lifted her head from the menu. I put my napkins aside and leaned onto the table. We all glued our eyes on Dillon, awaiting a response. He wiped sweat from his forehead.

"I can't tell them," he whispered, averting his eyes.

"Why not?" Chris leaned forward with a confused look.

"How could you leave your mother in the dark?" Sharon cocked her head in that peculiar manner of hers. I looked at Sharon and Chris. They probably both had mothers they could count on in times of need. My mother had left when I was only nine and died before I could see her again. But my situation had to be the exception. Maybe Dillon's mother would be there for him.

Dillon stared at the other coffeehouse patrons, chatting merrily over their steaming cappuccinos and mochas and lattes. They were oblivious to the fact that his world had collapsed, that he very well might not see his thirty-fifth birthday. The year was 1987 and there was neither a cure for AIDS nor anything that would delay the inevitable. He turned back to us, his pale blue eyes distant, lusterless, as if the life was already being sucked out of him.

"They don't know I'm gay," he muttered, his voice cracking.

I swallowed dryly. Sharon gawked in disbelief.

Chris, who was open about his homosexuality with both family and friends, couldn't make sense of this. "Don't you think it's time you told them?"

"I can't," Dillon replied with a pained expression. He refused to say another word about it.

I assumed, as we probably all did, that Dillon's mother would most likely not approve of his being gay, a clear reason for keeping it a secret up to this point. Yet, no matter what our personal experiences with our families, we all subscribed to the idealistic assumption that, regardless of the relationship, a mother, *any* mother would be able to cross that chasm and reach out to her dying child. While Dillon and Chris had been friends for some time, Sharon and I knew him only casually. None of us really knew how to deal with the situation, much less how to help Dillon. So we did the best thing we could think of: we encouraged him to contact his family for help. Almost two stressful hours and numerous mochas and lattes later, we succeeded.

"Thanks, guys," he said, across a graveyard of empty cups. He disappeared in the stream of customers.

* * * * *

A week or so later, I was sitting behind the counter at The Light Spot paging through a new book. Paul, a dark-haired young man with a disheveled look, sat at a table with tarot cards spread in front of him. A middle-age woman listened to his reading with wide eyes. Paul had offered to pay me a portion of the fees he received for his readings, but since he charged only ten dollars, I had declined. From his appearance, I suspected that he was living out of his car and badly needed the money. I also enjoyed learning about tarot and pagan spirituality from him.

The telephone rang.

"Patti? Is Chris around?"

"Dillon? No, he hasn't come in. No clients this morning, so maybe he went to the beach."

"I, ah...," he sniffled. His voice choked.

Anxiety gripped me. "Dill? What's the matter?"

"I told her. I called my mother and told her like you guys said."

"What happened?" I asked, twirling the telephone cord with one finger.

Moments passed with only soft sobs coming across the line. "She said she never wanted to talk to me again." He broke down.

I almost dropped the phone. Other than Chris, Dillon had no one to turn to. I sat up straight and squared my shoulders.

"Dillon, where are you?"

"Home."

"I'll be right over."

A wave of acid welled up in my belly as I sped to Dillon's apartment. I had no idea what I was going to say or do, just that I had to get there. Helping and counseling people was Chris's domain. I had always been so caught up in my own dramas and struggles that helping other people with their problems, aside from husband and immediate family, had never even been on my radar screen. Finding myself in this role now was miles away from my comfort zone.

I parked the car and headed up the steps, mulling over what Dillon had said on the phone. *She never wants to talk to him again? He probably didn't tell her he had AIDS – just that he was gay. That has to be it.*

Dillon was curled up on the couch in a fetal position, tears streaking his young face. My guts churned inside. I felt totally inadequate to this task. Where in the world was Chris?

I sat next to him on the couch. "What did she say?"

"She didn't want to listen. She got real angry when I told her I was gay. She kept yelling at me, saying I'm damned."

"You told her that you have AIDS?"

"I did. She didn't care. My family are fundamentalists."

My jaw dropped. How could a mother abandon her child in this situation? I remembered how Dillon had shut down when we asked him about his family at the coffeehouse. I cringed, recalling how I had joined the chorus that convinced him to contact his family. How could we have been so blind?

Nudging closer, I draped one arm across his shoulder. He curled up and wept.

"I'm scared, Patti. I don't want to die."

Finding no words, I enfolded him in a warm embrace. He laid his head on my shoulder as his body wracked with convulsions of grief. The moments stretched and bent and twisted, heavy with the weight of grief, of fear, of despair. And as I held this young man, having nothing else to offer him but the warmth of my two arms—sensing the weight of his head on my shoulders, the wetness of his tears on my blouse, the pounding of his heart against my chest—my heart began to flutter, shiver, *awaken,* flooding me with feelings and sensations I had no frame of reference for. The flutter became a shiver, the shiver a tremor, the tremor a virtual earthquake, shaking me down to the very foundations of my being. Until that moment, I had believed I understood the concept of compassion and unconditional love. I had studied Buddhist materials, listened to talks of the Dalai Lama, read books such as Gerald Jampolsky's *Love is Letting Go of Fear* and Leo Buscaglio's *Love,* had participated in Religious Science church services and A Course of Miracles groups, all advocating love and compassion for all of humanity. Yet, while I considered myself a caring human being, deep inside I still held to the belief system that I could only *truly* love a selected few, that there was a limited supply of my love to go around, that opening my heart to many human beings would make me vulnerable to hurt and attack.

I continued to hold Dillon in my arms, soothing him the best I could. Energy escaped my heart, undulating in waves; its fire scalding, blazing. As a fountain of energy flowed from my heart to his, I was overwhelmed with emotions so deep, so intense, so beyond my comprehension of *feeling* that my whole body shook. I shivered and my eyes brimmed with tears and I understood.

This was true compassion.

* * * * *

I have tried to fathom some meaning, some reasoning behind illness, especially painful and fatal disease. Does disease manifest in our lives because we have abused or neglected our bodies? Does it happen as a result of our negative thoughts and fears, compounded over the years until they finally manifest in physical form? Both of these were possibilities, but I believe there are also deeper layers than this. Would a soul *choose* to incarnate and attract a deadly or incapacitating disease to itself as part of its lesson, its growth, its mission and purpose? Could this also be part of the lessons for the people the soul interacts with?

Could this argument also extend to souls who incarnated into bodies or families or personalities that were different from the larger society in which they lived? *Maybe* the purpose of these souls, at the very least, is to teach people tolerance. *Maybe* their mission involves shaking people out of rigid belief systems to help open mind and hearts.

* * * * *

Shortly after Dillon checked into the hospital, Sharon burst into The Light Spot, her eyes blazing murderously. "Is Chris around?"

"He's with a client," I said. "Just went in."

"I can't believe these people," she hissed, her fists bunched. "They came, you know. They're with him right now, in the hospital, *torturing* him."

"Who?"

"Dillon's family. I walked into his room and there's this man standing at the foot of the bed, slapping a Bible, telling Dill he's a sinner, telling him to repent! Dillon looked horrified. I screamed at the man, asked him what he thought he was doing."

"What happened?"

Sharon's voice rose. "They called security and had me removed from the hospital. They're his family – four of them. They, according to the hospital staff, have the right to decide for him. Have the right to be with him. I tried to explain to the nurse what they were doing, but it fell on deaf ears. Apparently, friends have no rights."

I felt a twitch in my left eye. Sharon plopped down on a wooden chair. I served her a cup of coffee.

"Why would they show up now?" I asked.

"The social worker at the hospital convinced them to come. How could she know they'd be this way?" She sipped her coffee. "By the way, before the hospital security arrived, Dillon asked me for a small tape player so he could play soothing music. But I couldn't get it to him, couldn't go back. Can you believe that family of his?"

"I have one. I'll take it to him."

* * * * *

I approached Dillon's hospital room with caution, the small Sony tape player in tow. The family members sat in a row to one side of the hospital room, protective blue masks covering their faces, expressions cold and grim. They had positioned themselves as far away from Dillon as they could get, as if he were an *untouchable*, like the Dalits of India or the Burakumin of Japan. As if he were too impure, too polluted, too foul to be worthy of human emotions.

"I'm a friend of Dillon's," I said as I stepped into the room. They nodded, eyeing me suspiciously.

"You're supposed to wear a mask," one woman said.

"That's okay." *They're probably more worried about themselves than Dillon.*

The brother-in-law stood over Dillon's bed with a Bible, slamming his palm against it every few seconds with a loud thump. "Do you repent your evil ways? Do you ask the lord for forgiveness?" he demanded from behind his blue mask.

Dillon glanced at me, his eyes filled with pain. Heat rose to my face. *Would Jesus treat a dying person like this?* I thought, grinding my teeth with anger. Yet my defiance would have to be subtle; otherwise, I'd meet the same fate as Sharon.

To the shock and disbelief of his family, I leaned over and touched Dillon, greeting him with a gentle hug. "I've brought the tape player you asked for, Dill. Where do you want it?"

"On the table, right here. My tapes are in the drawer," he said, struggling to control the quavering in his voice.

I busied myself setting up the tape player. The brother-in-law paused, Bible in hand, a spasm of irritation crossing his face. The rest of the family glowered at me from across the room. Pulling up a chair, I sat next to Dillon, held his hand, and focused on sending kind, loving feelings to him. The Bible-thumper stood at the foot of the bed and continued with his rhetoric. The leather jacket of his Bible was worn, cracked; his expression stern, unforgiving. *Is this all these people can muster up to give of themselves?* My heart went out to Dillon.

Yet Dillon took whatever they threw at him. He did not ask them to leave. He did not request help neither from me nor the hospital staff. Maybe he needed his family there to give him a sense of belonging, regardless of their behavior. Maybe he understood that acceptance of his homosexuality was a journey they could not make. Maybe he understood that trying to "save his soul" was their way of expressing their love for him, their bizarre way of saying that they cared.

Squeezing his hand gently, I rose to leave. "I'll be back, Dill," I whispered in his ear. He managed a whisper of a smile in response.

As I reached the door of the hospital room, I turned back and glared at the family members, shaking my head in the manner I do when I'm confounded by people's behavior. They responded with blank stares.

* * * * *

Later that afternoon, I spilled out the events of the day to Chris in one breathless jumble. His face hardened. "Let's go see him," he said, grabbing my hand and taking off towards the hospital, just a few blocks away.

It was dusk. The family members had left. The dim room smelled of impending death and despair. A cold sweat had beaded on Dillon's pale face. Chris did not hesitate. He pulled the covers aside, climbed into the bed, and embraced Dillon, providing a loving space for his ill friend to release pent-up emotions. I watched silently, my heart wrenching, as Dillon wept in Chris's arms.

Fifteen or twenty minutes later, Dillon was calm, his face serene. Chris slid out of the bed and gently tucked him in. I kissed Dillon on the forehead and took my leave.

Chris and I visited Dillon several times in the next few weeks, attempting to calm him, showing him that we cared.

It was early evening on that final visit, the hospital corridor dark and depressing. Chris and I entered Dillon's hospital room, and stopped, frozen in place.

His bed was empty.

* * * * *

Even though I had not been close to Dillon, his death had shocked me like I'd been hit with a lightening bolt.

On some level, I knew that the tough experiences of life are there for a purpose, to help us learn and grow and evolve; that I needed to look for the gift in all of this. Nevertheless, this knowledge doesn't make the experience less excruciating to endure.

As time passed, my heart slowly soothed and healed. But it was months after Dillon's death that his true gift began to manifest itself. My experience with Dillon had cracked opened my heart and it began to blossom, softly, petal by petal, with strange, new, wonderful emotions and sensations coursing through my veins and bubbling to the surface. What were these feelings and emotions? Could they be the *compassion* of the Buddhists, the *love of* the Christians, the *rapture* of the Sufis? My skin tingled, as if had been in stasis for years and had just come back to life. I could sense my spirit reaching out to me, touching me—I could hear it in my mind, feel it in my heart. Was this, the opening of the human heart, the true path to awakening? Consider:

- In Hinduism, it is believed that divinity permeates all things, including the human heart. One's purpose in life is to discover a path to experience this divine essence directly.

- *The Course in Miracles* states: "Know thyself; there is nothing else to seek."

- Jesus of Nazareth said: "…before kingdoms change, the hearts of people must change."

- The Sufis, the mystics of Islam, become enraptured with the love of God whom they call the *Beloved*.

PETER

My friend Chris and I spent a great deal of time together. We organized and ran *Course of Miracles* study sessions and group rebirthings at the Inner Visions Center, discussed spiritual concepts and ideas over steaming cappuccinos in the Light Spot, savored the food in the many restaurants and cafés in the Hillcrest area, attended Sunday meetings at the Church of Religious Science, and participated in various seminars and workshops on personal growth and transformation. We enjoyed watching videos, going to the movies, and traveling along with other friends. He liked to take me shopping, claiming that I dressed too "matronly" and I needed a more youthful look. He also recommended his favorite hair dresser to give me a modern cut and convinced me that I should have lighter hair. Playing hairdresser, he eventually transformed me into a blonde.

At the same time, my husband, Bahman, busied himself working at the copy center or playing volleyball and card games with his Persian friends. The changes in my physical appearance, my excitement and enthusiasm with my spiritual journey, and my desire to spend so much time with Chris dumbfounded him. And even though Chris was gay, I could sense that Bahman was not comfortable with this new development. Our lives had taken different roads and the gap between us was widening.

While having close friends may be the norm for many people—my sisters are quite the social animals, with a large circle of friends—it does not come easily to me. In fact, Chris had become the closest friend I'd ever had since my childhood friend and mentor, Ed.

Then, one day, Chris fell in love.

Suddenly, Chris had little time for me. He was going out with *Peter*. He was going to *Peter's* house. He was having dinner with *Peter*. Going to the movies with *Peter*. Having fun with *Peter*. Several weeks passed. *Peter* became my enemy.

Peter was a well-dressed interior designer with a deep tan, big blue eyes, and a shaggy head of salt and pepper hair that became him. He had shown up at one of our Course in Miracles meetings and Chris was smitten. On one hand, I wanted my best friend to be happy, to enjoy a loving, romantic relationship with a partner. On the other hand, I was downright jealous. I just couldn't believe I was feeling this way. Hadn't I progressed far enough on my spiritual path to be beyond such petty feelings? My mind said that I was being ridiculous, but my emotions had a life of their own and would not listen to reason.

Each time I saw Peter, I greeted him with a forced smile while my insides felt so raw you'd think an alien was devouring me from the inside out. And when Chris incessantly talked about his new beau, it took a great deal of effort not to roll my eyes and sigh. My feelings did not escape Chris, so he attempted to spend more time with me at the Light Spot or arrange for the three of us to get together. I tried to adapt to the situation, without much success. I felt small and petty and alone.

One Friday afternoon, Chris, Peter, and I drove out of the city to attend the Whole Being Weekend, a yearly event held at one of the mountain camps near Julian, California. The Whole Being Weekend offers rustic housing or camping, vegetarian food, healing, connection with nature, and an array of mini-workshops for personal enrichment. During the drive, Chris chatted merrily with Peter. I slouched in the back seat like an angry child and watched the scenery go by.

Early Saturday morning, I was lying in bed, staring at the blank white ceiling, feeling like someone had stabbed me with a knife. I was going to have to get up, head down to the cafeteria, and meet Chris and Peter. Thinking of this created an excruciating pain in my midsection.

Help me God! Make the pain go away. I cried out in agony. *Tell me what to do.*

Silence. Moments passed with no reply. I took several deep breaths to calm body and mind. I knew from experience that whenever I was in a tense emotional state, it was very difficult to hear the voice of my spirit.

After a few minutes of deep breathing, I felt calmer, more open, more receptive. I asked again.

Make Peter your friend, came the soft whisper.

My friend?

Yes. Love him as you love Chris.

Hmph! I crossed my arms over my chest, lips pressed firmly together. I wanted the pain to go away. How would...

A light bulb suddenly turned on inside my head. *Oh, I see now. That makes sense.* I mulled over this idea for a while, trying to work through my resistance. *What if I changed my perspective? What if I saw him as a possible new friend, a second Chris. What if...* I smiled to myself. So many options, so many possibilities—and I had been seeing everything from such a narrow, limited view.

I popped out of bed, dressed in a hurry, and hustled down to the cafeteria.

Chris and Peter were sitting at a table waiting for me. I greeted them both warmly, kissed Peter on the cheek and seated myself. He looked startled. I beamed him my best smile.

Chris gawked in disbelief. Pulling himself together, he claimed that he had left something in the room and he'd return shortly. Peter and I sat in silence for a few awkward moments. I'd made my move. The ball was in his court. How would he react?

Peter eyed the food line. His face brightened. "Looks like it's getting shorter. Want to stand in line?"

I nodded.

As we walked up to the line, Peter wrapped one arm around me and drew me close. I pushed past my resistance and it felt good. His energy was familiar, comfortable. We stood in a warm embrace as if we were long lost friends who had just rediscovered one another.

Chris returned and, noticing Peter and me, stopped in his tracks. His face broke out in a smile.

* * * * *

That afternoon, Chris and I, along with other members of our rebirth team, held a group rebirthing in the lodge. The session had just concluded. Having released pent-up emotions, the participants were beginning to sit up on their blankets, a new sparkle and clarity visible in their eyes. I padded over to check on Peter who had been a participant. He was standing, his salt-and-pepper hair in disarray, his big blue eyes so intense, it was as if his very soul were peering out at me. Thanking me for the wonderful rebirthing session, he folded me in his arms.

My body shook, jolted, as an electric current snaked up my spine. I stumbled back and looked up at him, confused. "What did you just do?"

He smiled, but said nothing.

My skin tingled. I felt spacey, yet centered, like I'd been catapulted into a different state of awareness. The incessant chatter in my mind had come to a sudden stop.

"I have to go lie down," I whispered to Chris.

"Why, what's the matter?" he asked, a concerned look on his face.

"Not sure. Peter gave me an electric shock and I'm feeling all weird. I'll catch up with you later."

I lay on my bunk bed, feeling more open, more aware than I'd ever remembered. I was right there, in the moment, with no mind chatter. Dusk came and darkened the room and I realized that I had been completely oblivious to the passing of time. I recalled reading in Carlos Castaneda's books how Don Juan would smack Carlos in the middle of his back in order to shift his assemblage point and break him of his fixed mind set. Was this what Peter had done to me? I couldn't be sure, and, after questioning him, discovered that neither was he.

* * * * *

On the last day of the Whole Being Weekend, we were all invited into the meadow to participate in an exercise in trust. This involved choosing a partner and having that person lead you around the meadow, touching different objects with your eyes closed, then trading roles and repeating the exercise. Peter and I partnered for this experience. Closing my eyes, I let him hold my hand and guide me as I stumbled along, touching the petals of a flower, the leaves of a tree, the fur of a cat. Afterwards, we sat on the grass, soaking in the warm rays of the midday sun. I had opened to new levels of trust and felt at peace with myself and the world. No words were needed.

My inner pain had disappeared, and Chris, Peter and I became close friends. I had been seeing Peter as an enemy, as someone who was taking my friend from me. Once I opened my heart and changed my perspective, I changed my world.

The Heart of Compassion

While I had always considered myself a kind human being, I have a tendency to open up to only a selected few—family, close friends, husband—and not much further than that. The loss of my mother at a young age, coupled with the trauma of living in a culture I did not understand, had left me with a gaping hole inside, a black void that would suck me in unless I gave regular attention to my own needs and provided myself with constant love and care. As a result, I shielded my heart like a lioness protecting her cub. This didn't leave a whole lot of energy to spend on the rest of humanity.

But now, at thirty-six, things were changing. I lifted my eyes, looked beyond my own predicament, and noticed that there were other people in the world—people with pain and sorrows and struggles of their own. And my heart went out to them…

I began to change, transform—a new Patti emerged that even I did not recognize. Instead of constantly complaining about life, little by little, I began to feel and express gratitude for all the good in my life—my family, my friends, my work, and my health. Slowly, over time, I began to reach out to others: sending money to people hurt by natural disasters; throwing baby showers for colleagues who had no family nearby; distributing flowers at a retirement home; giving away items that I no longer needed to people who could use them; sharing small gifts of gratitude with those around me; taking people out to lunch—just because.

As my heart opened further, the still small voice of my spirit came to me more frequently and much more clearly. I realized that it is not the form of religion or tradition that we choose; it is through the awakened heart that we ultimately find God.

Chapter Eight: Follow Your Bliss

*We must be willing to let go of the life we have planned,
so as to have the life that is waiting for us.*

– Joseph Campbell

San Diego, California - 1988

Just back from a Hawai'i vacation, Chris burst into the Light Spot, his face lit up like a Christmas tree. "There's this little town, really quaint, on the Big Island," he explained, barely containing his enthusiasm. "It's called Hilo. Lush green, the air so soft and balmy it caresses your face. It would be a great place to live."

My stomach clenched. "Live in Hawai'i?"

"You have to go there, Patti. Just as you get off the plane, you experience this feeling of peace. You take a deep breath and inhale the air perfumed with tropical flowers, and you just know that you've arrived in Paradise."

I gawked at him in disbelief, struggling to digest this new information. "You really think you'll move to Hawai'i?"

"Yep, that's the plan," he said with a huge smile, then took off to tell other people about his newly found paradise.

I stood there like I'd been rooted to the floor, staring at Chris's back as he headed out the door. *Am I going to lose my best friend?*

I inhaled deeply, attempting to calm myself. *It's probably just a pipe dream. He was on a tropical island, had a great time, and didn't want to let it go. It must happen to a lot of people.*

But Hawai'i had gotten under his skin; he loved the lush green landscape, the warm ocean water, the soft tropical breeze. In the following days and weeks, he talked about it to anyone and everyone he met. He dreamed of owning land, growing organic foods, and living close to nature. His enthusiasm was working its magic on Peter, although Peter was still far from being convinced.

Sitting in the Light Spot with a warm cappuccino, I felt a knot constrict my throat at the thought of possibly losing Chris – the person who had introduced me to rebirthing and metaphysics, the man who had helped me through my quagmire of emotions, my partner in the Inner Visions Center, my best friend.

If he was serious about this move, I didn't see any option for me. I was teaching English as a Second Language at the community college. I managed The Light Spot and ran The Inner Visions Center. I had *family* in this town—my two younger sisters had followed me to San Diego several years before. They had gone to college, married, and had several children, my niece and three nephews. I was *married*. My husband, Bahman, was in business with my brother-in-law and doing well. Dropping everything and everyone and moving 3,000 miles away wasn't on my radar screen. And while I was intrigued by Chris's animated descriptions of Hawai'i, I didn't think, by any stretch of the imagination, that I would ever move there.

My spirit, however, had other plans.

* * * * *

A few weeks later, Chris, Peter, and I were hanging out in The Light Spot. The strong scent of brewed coffee filled the air. A slender woman sat at an adjacent table, flipping through a book on positive thinking. Two men with thinning hair perched on white plastic chairs out on the deck, talking merrily with their hands. Paul, his hair mussed up, his clothes crumpled as usual, was doing a tarot reading for a young woman who listened to him with wide eyes.

"This psychic woman I visit is really good," Peter said, grabbing my attention. He sipped on his café latte, then continued. "She's strange, though. Talks to a spirit named Angela who hovers in a corner near the ceiling."

"You go to a psychic?" I asked, grinning.

"Every once in a while."

Chris chuckled. "Sounds too weird to me. How do you know she's any good if she's telling you things that haven't happened yet?"

Peter shook his shaggy head of salt and pepper hair and fixed his big blue eyes on Chris. "I've been seeing her for several years now. A number of the things she's told me *have* come true. Besides, she only charges twenty dollars."

"Too strange for my taste," Chris said, dismissing the idea with a flick of his hand.

"Only twenty dollars, huh." I pulled up a chair while balancing a tiny cup of espresso in one hand. "Have you seen this spirit?"

"Nope, but she looks up into the corner of the room and asks the spirit questions." Peter's smile spread. "If nothing else, she's entertaining."

A psychic? Weird! But, then again, twenty dollars isn't much. Maybe I should open my mind and try new things. It can't hurt.

Pushing past my skepticism, I asked Peter for the information and made an appointment.

* * * * *

The psychic was an elderly woman, most likely in her seventies. She was plainly dressed in earthy colors, handmade shawl, dyed hair with white showing at the roots. But there was nothing plain about those piercing eyes. Their depth and intensity made me squirm.

I fidgeted in my seat, wondering what she was going to tell me. *Just relax. It's just for fun. Peter may think she's reliable, but I'll decide for myself.*

The old woman raised her gaze to the upper right hand corner of the room. She nodded her head, as if agreeing with the information she was receiving from an invisible spirit.

"Angela sees you on a beach. White sand. An ocean."

San Diego has lots of beaches. So?

"This beach is not here. It's far away. An island."

Island? I sat up straight. *Peter must have told her something.*

She asked the invisible Angela a few more questions as if to clarify some new information.

"I see a ring." Hazel eyes bored into me. "Accept it."

A ring?

"Do you mean a wedding ring?" I asked, confused.

She looked up to Angela, who she apparently believed was hovering near the ceiling, then replied. "Yes. When the ring is offered, accept it."

"But I'm already married." I leaned forward to display my ring finger with its plain gold wedding band. *See! The woman's just a charlatan.*

"What are you doing still married?" She gestured wildly, her voice rising an octave. "You were complete with him some time ago. There is another you need to meet."

I stumbled out of the psychic's apartment in a daze. *What was she talking about? True, Bahman and I had been moving apart in recent years, but divorce him? No way. The woman's nuts!*

The following day, I reproached Peter for recommending the old woman.

"Are you so sure she's wrong?" he said, a mischievous look in his eyes.

I shrugged off his comment without another word. I had no intention of leaving my husband.

* * * * *

A few months later, on a clear, sunny afternoon, I was standing on a San Diego sidewalk, waiting for the green light in order to cross the street when, without warning, my reality shifted and I found myself propelled to another place.

I walk down a path flanked by tropical flowers and bushes. I can feel the soft breeze caressing my skin. I hear birds chirping in the o'hia trees. I wave to my friends Chris and Peter, who have decided to stay on the beach. I enter a house with large, bright windows. I know this is my house. I know this is Hawai'i. A man approaches me. He is tall, with wisps of grey on the sides of his head. I cannot see his face. He embraces me, kisses me passionately. I am filled with love. I am happy!

Snap! Like a rubber band, I was pulled back to the present. My eyes flew open and I found myself back on the street corner in San Diego, the light beaming "walk" in bright green. Like an automaton, I obeyed, stumbling across the street and into my car. I leaned on the steering wheel in a daze. *What in the world was that?* It was not a memory, a stray thought, or a dream. The scent of plumeria, the sound of mourning doves, the sunlight filling the room, the warmth of the man's embrace. It had been so vivid, so real. Was this what they called a "vision"?

Over the ensuing weeks and months, these *visions* continued to appear every so often, at random, without warning. I wasn't sure what to make of this new development, but decided to pay attention to what was being shown me and try to make sense of it all.

* * * * *

These visions compelled me into examining my marriage. Bahman and I had married in 1974. The following year, we made plans to return to the United States to continue our education, but the Iranian government would not let him out of the country since he hadn't served in the military. With no other recourse, we resigned ourselves to wait two more years until he completed his service and I continued teaching English at the Imperial Iranian Air Force. In August 1977, we moved to San Diego, California to pursue our studies.

The early years in the States were a financial struggle as we tried to put ourselves through college, but the sense of exploration and adventure was still alive. We took classes in world religions and mysticism; we read and discussed Carlos Castaneda's material.

After college, I began teaching English as a Second Language part time while pursuing a graduate degree in Linguistics. Bahman wasn't happy with his choice of anthropology major—he didn't seem to be making much headway and prospects for employment were slim. As a result, he dropped out of his master's program and went from job to job, never able to find his niche. Money was tight until the mid-eighties, when my sister's husband offered to make him a partner in his business.

As the years passed, the adventurous rebel in Bahman was transformed into a middle-aged man who spent all his time working, taking occasional trips to Las Vegas, playing volleyball or cards, or just hanging out with his buddies. He gradually became less willing to try new things, see new places, learn and change and grow. Meanwhile, I was spending more and more time away from home with my teaching job, my café and bookstore, and my friends Chris and Peter, constantly working on my spiritual development. Over time, my ideas, my beliefs, the way I saw the world, shifted and changed. My world was now a magical place overflowing with possibilities—a place where I could flex and grow and pursue my dreams. Bahman's world was unchanged—live and eat and play and die. Each time I tried to explain my new spiritual beliefs, he looked at me with confused eyes.

We were drifting apart, neither of us willing to admit it. We didn't fight. We didn't argue. We just each went our own way and did our own thing. Finally, in late 1988, my forty-year-old husband moved out of the bedroom and began sleeping on the futon couch. "I'm going through my mid-life crisis," he explained. I, on the other hand, was a thirty-seven-year-old going on twenty-one, just on the cusp of experiencing life.

I tried to think about the good times, the fun times: trips to the Caspian sea; evenings when Bahman used to strum the guitar and I joined in on the bongos; sleeping under the stars on hot summer evenings in Tehran; long walks in San Diego's Balboa Park; Iranian New Year's parties; our first trip to Disneyland; Christmas at Nana's place in Florida; trips to San Francisco, Lake Tahoe, and Mexico. After fourteen years of marriage, I still loved my husband, yet I was coming to the realization that I needed to move on with my life and it felt like my stomach being put through a shredder

Lost and confused, with nowhere else to turn, I swallowed my pride, ignored my skepticism, and made an appointment with a second psychic, a prominent expert who was known for her high degree of accuracy.

"Moving to Hawai'i is your destiny," she said, firmly echoing the first psychic's predictions.

"But what about my husband?" My stomach fluttered.

She leaned forward, tenting her hands on the table. "You've been disillusioned with that marriage for some time now. You're going to have to admit it to yourself."

I stumbled out of her office, a jumble of mixed emotions. *Am I really disillusioned with my marriage? What do I really want or expect?* Bahman had always been kind, gentle, respectful—things I admired in a man. Yet, as I grew older, those qualities were not sufficient. And even though I had never consciously thought about it, deep down, I was beginning to realize that I wanted a man who was strong, capable, self-sufficient, a man who could succeed in this world; a man who knew who he was and what he wanted out of life; a person who saw life as full of possibilities rather than limitations; someone who I could depend on through thick and thin; a companion who wanted to create a home, set down roots, and be there for me in my elder years. I wanted a best friend with a passion for adventure and the courage to carry it out. I wanted a man who had never lost his sense of awe and wonder, that little boy inside. I wanted a man who made me laugh.

I recalled being diagnosed with cancer back in 1979. The initial wake-up called that had propelled me on the road to self-discovery. I remembered how I had clutched my husband's arm for support in the clinic, groping for his inner strength, finding nothing but sympathy and fear.

I remembered returning home from the doctor's office, only to receive another shock when Bahman seemed more worried about the bills than my dying. It was summer.

He was out of school and only worked a few hours a day. He *could* have gotten a temporary second job. He *could* have tried to allay *my* fears instead of adding to them. After the operation, Bahman had visited me faithfully every day in the hospital, but the moment I was home, I was left, feeling alone, abandoned.

I recalled the Thanksgiving visit in Florida back in 1983. How meeting Ed again had brought all the suppressed pain of my childhood to the surface, again propelling me on a journey of inner healing. I remembered reaching again for Bahman's inner strength, only to find confusion and fear. I had always been the rock in the relationship. Bahman did not know how to play that role. And while he was still loving and caring, I found that I could not depend on him for the support I needed. I was on my own.

These memories stung, like the venom of a wasp. Maybe Bahman had once been the man I wanted him to be, or I thought he could have become that person, but now, in his forties, he'd become complacent, confused, cautious. I had awakened, grown, changed. He had not. My heart wrenched at the realization—Bahman no longer made me laugh.

Could the psychic be right? I got into my car, barreled down the road, and headed up the California coast, trying to take in the salty ocean air, the breeze blowing my hair, but my stomach was clamped, nauseated. My eyes stung with tears.

After about an hour of driving, I pulled into a parking lot near an unknown beach. Plopping down on sparkling white sand, I stared vacantly out into the deep blues of the Pacific Ocean. A wave rolled in and stretched, tickling my toes. I scooted back and lay down on the sand, watching a puffy cloud hang lazily in the California sky, making a vain attempt at calming the knot in my stomach and the palpitations of my aching heart. Would I have to separate from my husband of fourteen years? Is this where my spiritual path was taking me?

* * * * *

Chris, still enamored with Hawai'i, insisted that I visit the Big Island, so I convinced Bahman that we both needed a vacation and made plans to visit paradise.

We played tourist on Oahu for a few days, snorkeling at Haunama Bay, browsing the shops of Waikiki, visiting Chinatown, and trying out ethnic foods. But something was missing. We both knew it. Felt it. It hung in the air between us like the stench of rotten meat.

I was restless. I craved spiritual food. Maybe it was an addiction of sorts—a need to get my regular dose of "feel good" juice. I searched the phonebook and scanned the paper. I discovered a place called The Aquarian Foundation, only a few blocks from our hotel in Waikiki. Though I had no information about this particular group, I figured it would be worth checking out. They offered a Wednesday night spiritual church service and healing. I smiled; it was Wednesday evening.

"They have a service tonight," I scribbled the address on a pad. "Will you go with me?"

"I don't want to," Bahman said with a tone of finality. He sprawled on the bed watching TV.

"Okay, I'll go by myself, then. See you later." His face told me that he was not happy, but he said nothing. I planted a kiss on his cheek and slipped out the door.

Weaving through the Japanese tourists down the streets of Waikiki, I was relieved to finally come across The Aquarian Foundation on Kuhio Street. My feet were aching. It had looked much closer on the map.

The door was wide open, so I stepped inside. A variety of small objects – stones, plastic disks, jewelry, arrowheads, and orange-colored rocks in different shapes— was displayed in glass cases. A tall, lithe woman with short blonde hair stepped up to the case and greeted me.

"These are apports," she said.

"Apports?"

"Objects materialized by our spiritual leader." She pointed to a photograph of a man with white substance flowing out of his hands.

While skeptical, I preferred to keep an open mind.

"What's that?" I asked, pointing to the white substance.

"It's called ectoplasm, a substance that our teacher produces when he goes into trance."

Ectoplasm manifested from the ethers? This place may be a little too far out for even my taste, but, what the heck, I'm here, I'll go along. I nodded to the woman in acknowledgement.

"The session is about to begin," she said with a smile.

I followed her into an adjacent room and took a seat with about twenty other people. The blond woman stepped up to the podium, welcomed everyone, than began a short talk. I'd thought that she was just a participant, but as she spoke, the energy in the room shifted, lightened. I sensed the space filling with non-physical beings, *light* beings, taking positions around the room, enveloping the participants in a semi-circle. While I couldn't actually see them, other than brief glimpses of gauzy images from the corners of my eyes, I *sensed* they were there.

"We have a guest from out of town," announced the speaker, looking straight at me. I felt a rush of heat in my face. "Would you like to come up to the podium and speak?" she asked.

The participants all turned, eyes glued on me. I swallowed dryly and rose from my seat, clasping and unclasping my hands. *What am I going to say? I don't know these people. I don't know this organization. I have no idea what they believe in.*

I reached the podium and faced the audience. Anxiety stabbed my gut. I gave them my name, told them I was visiting from San Diego, said I was happy to be there. *Maybe that will be enough.* I looked around the room and sensed the many non-physical beings, waiting, watching.

I felt an inner nudge, an urge, to publicly acknowledge them. *I can't do that. I don't know what these people believe in. They'll think I'm crazy!*

Silent seconds passed. I gazed out at the upturned faces in the audience, sensing their expectancy. The hazy images around the room became clearer, watching, waiting. The inner nudge became a push. My hands were wet and clammy. Sweat beaded on my forehead and dripped down my face.

"I don't really know if you believe in such things," I finally blurted out, my face so hot I thought I was on fire. "But there are many light beings in this room, standing all around." I gestured around the room. The participants nodded, their faces brightening.

"We do believe in them." The speaker beamed.

* * * * *

After the service, the speaker, a minister in this organization, asked if she could meet with me again. I was not sure why she was showing interest in me since I didn't live in Honolulu and would obviously not be returning, but she seemed like a pleasant enough woman, so I gave her the name of my hotel and room number.

She called the next day and we arranged to meet at the Ward Center, a shopping area in Honolulu. Bahman grudgingly agreed to come.

Over lunch, she said that she had called her spiritual teacher in Seattle and told him about me. *Why would her spiritual teacher want to hear about me?*

"He said that you had important work to do and that a being named Emil would like to work with you. He will be your guide for a time."

Emil. I remember reading that name in a series of books titled Life and Teachings of the Masters of the Far East. *I wonder if this is the same Emil.*

The speaker paid for our lunch and hugged me warmly before she left.

Bahman and I were driving back to our hotel. "I wonder who Emil is, what he's going to teach me." I was fascinated with the idea that a spiritual teacher had sent me this message.

"How do I know?" he replied flippantly. "I'm not metaphysical."

The following day, we flew from Honolulu to Hilo, a quaint town on the east side of the Big Island—the same town that had so enamored Chris during his visit.

"Let's just stay at the hotel," Bahman insisted. "I don't want to keep driving all over the place. It's tiring. I want to relax."

But I hadn't come all this way to hang out in a hotel. "Well, I can drive."

"No. I need to rest."

"But I want to see the island. You sure you want to stay here?"

He was adamant. I shrugged, grabbed the keys and took off. I drove up the Hamakua coast and turned onto the Four Mile Scenic Drive, a few miles north of town. The tropical vegetation was vibrant, alive, practically jumping out to grab my attention. I breathed in the clean air and reveled at the beauty of the waterfalls.

I continued up the coast. Cane fields sloped down to the deep blues of the Pacific Ocean. I explored a quaint town called Honokaa, then joined a few other tourists on a jeep tour down to Waipio Valley. We drove on mud roads through virgin forests and across clear streams. On the coast, white waves crashed over black sand and lava rock cliffs. Stray horses roamed through a grove of ironwood trees. Paradise found.

I returned to the hotel at dusk. Bahman, bored from hanging out at the hotel by himself, was now more than willing to venture out and explore the island with me.

The following morning, the warm island breeze blew my hair about as we drove up to Akaka Falls. The sky was a cerulean blue, a sharp contrast to the smog-covered southern California sky. A few puffy clouds hung like cotton candy waiting to be scooped up by a five-year-old. The ocean looked deep and velvety, the landscape brimming with life. I stepped onto the path leading to the falls, breathing in the perfumed air, my skin soft and moist.

I had taken but a few steps down the path when my awareness shifted and my skin began to tingle. I felt light as air, expanded, as if I'd been meditating for hours. I no longer walked on the path, I glided. Vibrant pink, white and magenta impatiens dotted the lush green vegetation along the walkway. I strolled past philodendron vines, wild orchids, and bamboo groves. The rainforest trees swayed in the breeze as if bowing, welcoming me. I had a strong sensation of having been there before. I felt connected to the earth, the plants, the water. I felt like I had come home.

"I'm feeling strange, like I barely have weight," I said to Bahman.

He shook his head, a baffled look on his face.

You will live here, a voice whispered in my ear. *For a time, but not your entire life.*

I plopped down next to a large tree to get my bearings, my skeptical mind in full gear. *Who is talking to me? The trees? The nature spirits? My angel guides? The spirit of the island? How can I be sure I'm not making it all up?*

I tried to explain to Bahman what was happening to me, but his expression told me I wasn't making much sense. Holding on to the large tree for support, I stood up, then froze in place, gawking at a carving in the tree trunk.

"What's the matter now?" Bahman asked, irritation evident in his voice.

My mouth wouldn't function, but I managed to point at the carving. Bahman's gaze followed my finger. For several moments, we both stood, mesmerized, like we'd just viewed Medusa and had been turned into stone. The carving clearly spelled out "Emil."

* * * * *

We drove in complete silence for a while, each trying to make sense of the experience.

"I'm going to move to Hawai'i," I said, breaking the silence. "I'm not sure when."

Bahman kept his eyes glued to the road, unresponsive.

"You can come later, when you're ready." My chest felt heavy, like I'd been poured into a mold of cement. The rift between us was now a chasm. We both knew that he would not be moving to Hawai'i. We both knew that our marriage was coming to an end.

* * * * *

Over the next eighteen months, Chris, Peter, and I took several trips to the Big Island of Hawai'i investigating, exploring, and having fun. We stayed in a log cabin up in the hills of Ahualoa; a coffee plantation on the Kona coast; a secluded B&B with magnificent views down in Puna; and watched the moon come up over the ocean while we camped on black lava rock cliffs.

On these trips, Chris, outgoing and animated as usual, chatted with everyone we met and discovered places the average tourist would normally miss. We soaked in a warm pond heated by a volcano, hiked through the back trails of Waipio Valley, discovered a black sand beach where bathing suits were optional, explored natural steam vents, and dined at a tucked-away Japanese restaurant overlooking the Waialea River. We inhaled the clean, perfumed air, splashed in the gentle ocean waves, reveled in the lush tropical plants and flowers, enjoyed the warm, balmy weather, and hiked in volcanic forests with gigantic ferns and o'hia trees.

In contrast to Chris's passion and outgoing personality that sparked and crackled like fire, Peter had the quality of air, flowing, ethereal, as if he had one foot in this world and the other in the world of spirit, and could pass through the veil at his choosing. We meditated on secluded cliffs, white waves crashing far below. When meditating with Peter, Chris and I could sense our energies quickly shift and lighten, sliding us gently into altered states of consciousness.

On one trip, we drove through Waimea, in the north of the island. Cows grazed lazily on green pastures while the cool mist created a surrealistic landscape.

"Look, a geodesic dome," Chris cried, turning the car towards the hills.

Peter and I craned our necks to see.

"I've read about them. About Buckminister Fuller. They're supposed to be easy to build. Sturdy. Let's go check it out."

After some maneuvering, we finally found the domed house. Chris parked the car and got out.

"What are you doing?" Peter asked, a tinge of alarm in his voice.

"I'm going to talk to the owners. Ask them about building a dome house. See what it's like to live in one," Chris replied, matter-of-factly.

"You're just going to walk up to a stranger's house, knock on the door, and ask them questions about their house?" Peter said, shaking his head.

Chris chuckled. "There *are* no strangers. Everyone's God."

To Peter's and my disbelief, he found the owners, introduced himself, and carried on an animated discussion for quite some time. Giving them warm hugs, he returned to the car.

"They love it," he said with a broad smile. "Something to think about."

The beauty and tranquility of the island had captivated all three of us. We talked about buying property and moving there together, although we did not have enough money to do so at the time. Nevertheless, we firmly believed that if we were meant to be there, God would open doors.

<u>Exploring Past Lives</u>

I sat behind the counter in The Light Spot, reading the last page of *Ecstasy is a New Frequency – Teachings of the Light Institute* by C. Griscom. In the book, Griscom talks about the spiritual healing process she uses to facilitate the recollection and experience of past incarnations. According to Griscom, when we access and then release the true source of negative imprints from other lifetimes, our karmic energy is freed and the healing process begins. This healing unblocks our connection with our spirit selves.

My mind felt like it had become elastic and it was being stretched in different directions. *And so, once again, we step into the Twilight Zone.* True, I had bought into the concept of reincarnation, at lease on an intellectual level, but to actually see and experience my past lives? Mind-boggling.

Chris, standing at the door of the Light Spot, said goodbye to a client and turned to me. "By the look on your face, I guess you've been reading the Griscom book."

I nodded.

"Just imagine," he said as he made us a couple of cappuccinos, "you can let go of patterns you've been holding on for lifetimes. Now *that* would be progress."

If it's possible. If it's real.

He placed the steaming cups of cappuccino on a table and I pulled up a chair. We sipped our brews and discussed the process and its implications. Much of our work towards spiritual enlightenment had involved letting go of negative core beliefs and patterns that we had picked up earlier in life. But what if we had patterns from past lives? Patterns and beliefs that were blocking our path to enlightenment. Was it possible to be free of them?

Chris drained the last of his coffee and set the cup down. He raised one eyebrow and stretched his lips into a broad grin. "Let's find out!" He popped up like a Jack-in-the-box, grabbed the phone from behind the counter, and called the Light Institute in Galisteo, New Mexico. After an animated discussion, he finally hung up and turned to me, his shoulders sagging, a hang-dog expression on his face. "It's expensive," he said through pouty lips. We slumped in our chairs in silence. It was not within our budget to experience this process, or so we thought at the time.

* * * * *

A week or so later, Chris swaggered into the Light Spot with his new client, Daniel, a young man in his thirties with a soft, serene face. "Daniel has gone through the process at the Light Institute," Chris explained, his face beaming.

I poured us all coffee and pulled up a chair to listen. Not only had Daniel completed the process at the Light Institute, he also facilitated this process for others. He made it very clear that he had *not* been trained nor was he endorsed by the Light Institute. In spite of this, the synchronicity of events was too perfect. Chris and I were so excited we couldn't stay in our skins.

Chris was the first to complete the process. "You meet with him four evenings in a row, three to four hours each session," he said, his face beaming. "And, guess what? Peter's going to do it, too."

"Did you actually see your past lives?"

"Yep! Clear as day."

"Did he use hypnosis?"

"No. He didn't hypnotize me at all. That's the interesting part."

"Then what did he do?"

He furrowed his brow and scratched his head. "To tell you the truth, I'm not really sure."

Is this possible? Can I really experience my past lives? While I believed Chris, I just had to find out for myself, so I called and set up an appointment with Daniel.

Past Life Viewings – May 1989

We sat on the carpet in Daniel's San Diego apartment, the street traffic a distant hum. *Here I go again, stepping right into bizzaro world. How do I get myself into these things?*

Daniel asked me to talk about my day. I babbled about this and that, all the while fighting the tension in my gut about the upcoming process. *This is all just a bunch of hooey. I'm delusional.* Nevertheless, I chatted away as if I needed to fill up the void. Daniel sat cross-legged on the carpet, listening.

My babble came to a sudden halt. My arms, my face, my whole body had started to tingle. I felt my eyes widen. "What are you doing?"

"Nothing."

"Then what is this tingling I'm feeling?"

"You're Higher Self is getting you ready for the process. You're almost there."

How can he tell?

"Am I really going to see my past lives?"

Daniel grinned widely. "It really doesn't matter what you believe you've seen. You can think of them as past lives, parallel lives, or visions created by your Higher Self to help you deal with belief systems that no longer serve your greater good. What's important is what you get out of the process."

I nodded.

Daniel guided me to an adjacent room and asked me to lie down on a massage table. I climbed on the table and made myself comfortable while he set up a tape player to record the session. My energy buzzed like the whirring of a bee hive.

Daniel attempted to calm me with his soft, soothing voice. I breathed in quick, short gasps, my heart doing flip flops. *What if I don't see anything?*

"Ask your Higher Self about the entity in the room with us this evening," Daniel said.

I took a deep breath. Heat rushed to my head. I knew exactly who it was. "It's the spirit of my mother."

"Why is your mother here at this time?"

I sensed my mother communicating with me. "She is here to support me. She also wants to view a past life with me. A life we shared together." *She's here! She's never shown up in spirit form before, or at least not that I know of.*

"Very well. Now ask your Higher Self to take you to a life that you need to see at this time."

Nothing, nada, only the blank, dark backs of my eyelids. Anxiety stabbed my gut as I sensed a part of me reaching out, grabbing, pulling.... Images attempted to form, but like gauzy spirits, were unable to coalesce.

"I can't see, can't make them out. It's all blurry!" I cried.

"Take a deep breath and relax."

I followed his directions. My anxiety dissipated.

"Good. Now ask your Higher Self to make the images clearer to you."

The darkness turned to gray; hazy images began to take form, more vivid, more real. And then they came, fast and furious—a deluge of images like a film on fast forward—a movie I was both watching and acting in it at the same time.

"Please describe what you are seeing and what you are experiencing," Daniel said, his voice seeming far away.

"I'm a little boy. I'm playing in a cave with a girl, slightly older. The cave feels safe, feels good. This is very long ago, prehistoric times."

"Can you describe yourself?"

"Messed up hair, smudges all over. Big smile. Green eyes. Brown hair. Totally naked, about five or six."

"And how do you feel about this life?"

"I'm totally happy and content."

"What is your relationship with your mother?"

"This is the mother of this lifetime, the same person. I go to her when I need her; otherwise, she lets me do whatever I want. She spends her time finding food for herself and me. She lets me be. This is the same relationship we had this lifetime. She just let me be. She was there to raise me to a point where I no longer needed her. This was her purpose, in both lives. She raises me until I'm fifteen. I have my spear and I can forage for myself now. I don't need her anymore, so I leave."

"Very well. Now ask your Higher Self to take you further in that life and explain what you are seeing and what you are experiencing."

I paused, trying to make sense of the images flickering through my mind. "I'm wearing a mask with a long wig of sorts, performing ceremonies like a shaman. I'm throwing things in the fire. The fire crackles. I learn to trust in the flow of spirit through ritual. I connect with spirit and learn to heal. I have great respect from others of my tribe. They come for my healing powers. I don't use herbs for healing, but prefer feathers and stones with specific qualities. I've had no teacher. I learned from the inner teacher. There was no seeking outside of myself. I opened and allowed the information to come through."

"Ask your Higher Self to take you forward in that lifetime," Daniel said, his voice soothing, encouraging.

In my mind's eye, I see an older man, his hair long and matted, his face determined. "I'm climbing a mountain to a temple, or a temple-like spot. I want quiet. I want to connect with Spirit, far away on the mountain. I have done my job, fulfilled my purpose for that lifetime. I want to be alone now. I want to be able to connect and just be."

"What about your mother?"

"I never saw her after I left at fifteen. I always wondered what became of her." I pause, listening to the message given me. "I'm being told that after I left, she was taken by a man and lived her life out with him. She was content." *Maybe I needed to leave. Maybe if I'd stayed, she would have never met that man.*

"Ask your Higher Self to take you to the time just before your passing from this lifetime."

The images shift, change. I see the man sitting in lotus position in a temple that overlooks a valley far below. "I pass out of this life by choice, high in the mountain temple. Sitting in meditation, I rise out of my body. My lifeless body remains sitting until people find it."

"Ask your Higher Self what the purpose of that life was."

I listen. The words come easily now, pouring into my consciousness. "She says that the purpose was for me to know that I can access all knowledge within myself and to release the fear of death, knowing that it is an illusion. My purpose was also to feel the joy of sharing and giving as I healed people."

"And your mother?"

I sense my mother's energy, close by, embracing me. I feel her love, her sadness. "My mother is still here. She wants me to know that when she was alive, in this lifetime, she had a great deal of guilt about leaving me, but once my father took me to Iran, it was too late. She had lost contact."

"And now?"

"Now she understands that she had to leave. It was our agreement. A sacred contract of our souls. She served me this lifetime by letting me go, because I needed the experiences I'd had in Iran, experiences my soul had planned. She has seen this lifetime with me. She has seen the karmic perfection, how I had to leave her in that lifetime and she had to leave me in this one. It's all a game. It's all a dance. All part of the divine plan."

My eyes swelled with tears. "She says that she really loved me and missed me all those years that we were separate. She wanted me to know that. She also wants me to know that she will be there to assist me when it is time for me to cross over." I let out a sigh as the heaviness in my chest lightened, expanded. A whisper of air brushed my face and the spirit of my mother was gone.

"I would like you to take a deep breath, releasing this lifetime, knowing that you have learned and grown from this experience."

I breathed deeply and let go…

* * * * *

I saw lifetime after lifetime during the four evening sessions, each one providing me with a profound insight into my own psyche, each one teaching me a lesson I needed to learn, a truth I needed to embody. I saw and experienced them like I was on a Star Trek halo deck. Were they past lives? Figments of my imagination? Lessons I needed to learn through vivid, graphic images? I honestly cannot say, but I'll share a summary of several others:

Egyption Priestess

It's ancient Egypt. I'm a female with long hair, white gown, lots of jewelry-- a priestess in the temple of Isis. I'm with two other priestesses preparing for ceremony. We sit around a crystal ball, touching it with the palms of our hands. One priestess is older, more knowledgeable, a princess of Egypt. We are oracles, blending our energies to receive information from the spirit world. We have increased our oracle powers by joining our energies, but the princess wants more. She convinces me and the other priestess to sacrifice ourselves, then assist her from the other side.

This sacrificial killing is done with a special dagger. During the ceremony, I have uncertainties, not sure why I agreed to this. I have fears that there is no spirit world and I will cease to exist, but I do not want to dishonor myself, so I swallow my fears and go through with it.

After our deaths, the princess calls to us. We decide that there is something evil about her and refuse to tell her anything. The princess is furious, outraged. She throws her fists in the air and screams. We giggle at her outburst. She cannot harm us now, so we leave that plane.

The lesson of this viewing is that I must always be true to my inner self, my own inner teachings, my own truth. I should follow the directions of my own spirit and never allow myself to be manipulated by another in any form. I should never trust what someone tells me just because they appear to be a great spiritual teacher or guru or have all knowledge or because of friendship or love or loyalties. It's about being true to my own inner self.

SLOT MACHINE WINNER

I'm a young man with dark hair, in my twenties. My clothes are not modern, but not ancient. This is France. I'm playing a slot machine and I win the jackpot—a substantial amount of money. The bells are ringing. I'm excited. They bring the money to me. I look at the money and feel undeserving. I did not work for this money, did not earn it. I believed that I needed to do something to receive this money. To earn it in some fashion.

There is a girl with me. Her name is Jacqueline. I am telling her about the money I won. She is excited. We plan a trip, an adventure, and book passage on a boat to America.

In San Francisco, we are swindled out of our money. I have to work hard the rest of my life to get it back. We do not lack, but we have a very ordinary existence. By the time of my death, I have finally accumulated some wealth. I want to give this wealth to my wife, Jacqueline. But she doesn't want the money. She says all she ever wanted was me. I had been so busy trying to recreate our wealth, I was left with little time to spend with her. Now, on my death bed, she doesn't even want it.

The lesson of this lifetime is that I was given money freely from the universe, yet I lost it because I felt unworthy and undeserving. Because I did not have the consciousness of money. I need to know that my feelings, my thoughts, and my beliefs attract money and objects to me; that God is my source and everything on the physical plane is just an avenue. I must understand that if I have the consciousness of money and deservingness that I can attract anything I need or desire in my life, that this does not require striving and struggle, unless I believe it to be so. It's all about consciousness. It's all about belief. I deserve abundance because I am a child of the universe, not because of who I think I am or what I do. I deserve it because I AM.

<u>Bastard Child</u>

I'm a baby boy. It's long ago, I'm not sure of the time period. My parents are arguing. My father says he has to leave, travel to other cities to play his music in the courts. He says he will be back, but right now he has to go.

Years have passed. I'm fourteen now. People are mean to me. They call me a bastard. I feel insecure, insignificant. I don't know who my father is. I don't even know his name. My mother refuses to give me any information about him.

This is a time when the value of a person is based on his lineage. Since I don't know my father, I'm a nobody. A reject. Life is difficult. I am afraid to approach people for fear of rejection or ridicule. I don't think I'm good enough for relationships of any kind.

I'm older—twenty-five. I leave the city, looking, searching. I heard that my father was a minstrel, although I have no name for him. I travel, searching the courts, asking the minstrels if they've had a child. None remember my mother.

For some reason, I don't blame my father for leaving. There was a love in my heart, looking for him, wanting to be with him. Wanting to know who he was. Feeling that somehow my self-identity was connected to who he was. To find my self-identity, I had to find him. I never did.

This lesson was for me to know and to understand that my self-esteem and identity are not in my physicality, but in the God within. The physical father merely symbolized my longing for God. I was feeling separate, disconnected. The pain and longing was for the connection with Spirit, not my physical father whom I didn't really know. And so I spent a lifetime searching for God outside of myself. The truth is, I don't have to look outside of myself to find divinity. It's with me. It's always been with me and belief in separation is nothing but an illusion. All I have to do is open and accept that. God is always with me, always there.

<u>Transformation</u>

During our first session, Daniel had directed me to make contact with my emotional being and my Higher Self. My emotional being had shown up as a white rabbit, hiding in the tall grass. My Higher Self appeared as the high priestess of the tarot deck wearing a gauzy blue gown, her face fuzzy and unclear.

Now that the past life viewings were complete, Daniel asked me to look for my emotional being and see if it had changed. I chuckled.

"What are you seeing?" he asked.

"The rabbit is growing, stretching. She's turned into a little girl with red hair, freckles, green eyes and braided hair. She's a character out of a movie. She's Pippi Longstocking!"

"And what does Pippi Longstocking mean to you?"

"She can do anything she desires. Go anywhere she wants. She's very strong. For Pippi, there is no problem that can't be solved. For everything there is an answer."

"I would like you to embrace your emotional being," Daniel coached me.

I opened my arms. Pippi came close. We blended, melded. I felt her strength coursing through my veins. "She's no longer physically there. She's inside of me."

"And what about your Higher Self. Has she changed?"

"She still looks like the high priestess of the tarot deck, but her clothes are purple instead of blue. She sits on the grass, cross-legged. I sit next to her."

"What about her face? Can you see her?"

I laughed out loud. "My Higher Self is me!"

I saw about sixteen lifetimes during the four-night session, and while this process may or may not have been similar to the one offered at The Light Institute, it was, for me, a major impetus for change. It helped me to deal with my outdated belief systems, change my perspective on many core issues, and create a new paradigm for my life.

I learned that I need to trust the small voice within rather than any outside authority; that God is my source and what I need and desire can come to me once I develop the consciousness that I deserve and accept my good; that it doesn't have to be hard work or struggle.

I became aware of the fact that life is not all what it seems, that our relationships with people and the events and challenges in our lives have a higher purpose, lessons to move us forward towards the growth of our souls and the fulfillment of our missions. And although I had worked much with Chris about forgiving and letting go of issues and resentments I held towards my mother, it was only after encountering her spirit and viewing a past life together that I truly understood. I was now at peace with this issue.

I discovered that death is an illusion and need not be feared; that our spirits are eternal; that the lives we lead are but a dance, a blip on the screen where we play a role in a movie called life.

I recognized that I have value because I am a child of God, because I have the spirit of God within me, not because of who my parents are, what I do, what I know, or what I look like. I understood that God was not some unreachable entity high in the heavens, but closer to me than the air I breathe, even closer than the drumming of my heart.

These substantial changes in my belief system registered on a core level, changing me in the most profound way—I felt lighter, happier, more at ease with myself and the world, as if a heavy load had been lifted from my shoulders. I knew I had changed, shifted my vibration. I could feel it in my bones. It was only a matter of time until my outer reality also changed.

* * * * *

Life at home in San Diego was becoming unbearable, the energy thick, sticky, like sitting in a barrel of molasses. Bahman and I became more uncomfortable around each other, so we avoided one another as much as possible, returning home only to sleep. We knew it was over, yet the reality of it was too hard to face. We were stuck.

In late May, Chris and Peter came to my rescue and asked me to move in with them. Bahman did not protest. And so, on July 1st, 1989, I left my husband and moved into my friends' home on Coronado Island. A new life and adventure had begun.

Chapter Nine: The Power of Letting Go

Trying creates impossibilities, letting go creates what is desired.

—Stalking Wolf, Hopi Elder

Dry leaves crunched under my feet as I sauntered up the forest path towards the lodge at The Whole Being Weekend retreat near Julian, California. This year, Chris had planned to conduct the rebirthing session again along with the team he had personally trained, yet the day before the retreat, he was in a cranky mood. "Why do I always have to be responsible for everything," he'd said, throwing up his hands. "There are plenty of trained rebirthers. I'm not going." He'd stomped out of the house without another word.

I felt as if I had been drenched with a pot of cold water. *Maybe he's just feeling burned out. He's offered this free group rebirthing several times.* But these rationalizations didn't help much. I kicked a pile of leaves and dirt up in the air, watching them float down to the path. *I don't need him,* I mumbled through clenched teeth as I marched up to the lodge.

The rebirthing session, a major event of the Whole Being Weekend, was held at two o'clock. The participants trickled into the lodge early, pillow and blanket in tow, milling about to find a spot. The rebirth team members, dressed in their bright pink T-shirts with turquoise letters that spelled out: The Inner Visions Rebirth Team, directed and assisted the participants. I stood in the front of the room, chewing on my lip. Chris had said he wasn't coming, although a part of me still clung to the idea that he would step through the door any minute, surprising us all. The room had filled to capacity, row after row of participants, sitting or lying on their blankets, waiting, watching, all eighty-two of them.

Five minutes past two, I peeked out the door. No one was in sight. Sweat trickled down my face, down my back, down my ribcage. I looked at the other rebirthers, pleading for direction. One shrugged his shoulders. Another shook his head. A third cracked his knuckles.

Time stretched. The participants became fidgety, impatient. A couple of the rebirthers looked in my direction. I whispered to one that I would begin. He circled the room, informing the others.

I explained the rebirthing process, trying to drag it out a bit. It was now fifteen minutes past the start time. I swallowed, but the lump remained in my throat. My cheeks were on fire.

What should I do? I asked my inner spirit.
Lead.

What?
Lead the rebirthing session.
Me?
The others will assist you.
Can you help me?
If that is what you wish.

I took a deep breath to calm my roiling stomach and directed the participants to lie down. I had worked with individuals in private rebirthing sessions, but Chris had always led the groups while I assisted. I said a brief prayer, releasing the session to Spirit, then started the tape. A hush came over the room as the haunting sounds of Constance Demby's *Novus Magnificat* filled the space. My skin tingled, vibrated. My arms took on a life of their own, stretched out to either side, palms faced up, rising slowly with Demby's haunting voice and otherworldly sounds, as if I were lifting the energy of the room in harmony with the music.

The music reached a crescendo. My body pulsed, vacillated. I suddenly felt lightheaded, floaty, and had the odd sensation of not being in the driver's seat, like I was now the observer, watching my body perform the necessary tasks. *What is going on?*

The rebirth session was in full swing. I worked the room, helping people, softly touching their hearts, handing them tissues, breathing softly so that they stayed in the correct rhythm, connecting the inbreath to the outbreath.

My energy was buzzing. I found myself assisting people in ways that I'd never been taught. I could actually *see* people's blockages, like dark clouds or shadows, over parts of their bodies. Kneeling beside them, I used my hands and arms in spiral gestures to open chakras, waving motions to clear off energy, pulling motions to extract negativity. A part of me watched all this, wide-eyed and in awe. I wasn't sure what exactly I was doing, or what part of me was doing it, yet deep inside, I knew I was doing the right thing.

One rebirther shot me a questioning glance. Another whispered in my ear, "What are you doing?"

"I don't have the foggiest idea," I replied with a shrug. "This isn't me—I'm not the one doing it."

He shook his head in puzzlement as he gently stepped over a participant.

A large, heavy-set man began to thrash around on his blanket. I glanced in his direction, sensing a "stuckness" to his energy. I intuitively knew he needed help.

Tiptoeing over to the man, I knelt next to him. His face was contorted, as if in deep emotional pain. Gently sliding my hand under his head, I urged him to sit up, then wrapped my arms around him and held him close to my heart. His chest heaved and his eyes swelled with tears. Soon the pain poured out of him in loud groans, sobs, convulsions, and tears. I held onto him the best I could, considering I was less than half his size. Another rebirther handed him some tissues. When he finally calmed, I gently directed him to lie down and continue breathing. He appeared more relaxed, more at peace, his breathing rhythmic and clear.

Two hours later, the rebirthing session ended and, after sharing some of their experiences, the participants emptied the room. I stumbled out into the crisp mountain air and headed towards my cabin, my heart pounding. *What had just happened?*

Reaching my cabin, I curled up under a blanket, shivering and in awe at what I had just experienced. I realized that my ego or personality self had stepped aside during the session and a much older, wiser, more experienced "me" had taken over, that spiritual part of me that has all knowledge and did what was necessary to help people let go of their negative energies and emotions.

Chris showed up later that evening. He gave no clear explanation why he'd refused to come in the first place, but he'd heard that the rebirthing session had gone well and he took great pride in the fact that his protégé had taken charge. My anger dissipated and I smiled. I just couldn't stay mad at Chris.

Looking back at this event, I recall that I had clearly asked Spirit for help. During those two hours, I did not have to think or struggle or try to remember anything. I had no fear and no worries. I intuitively knew what to do and accomplished each task with ease and grace. While I have never, since then, had such a clear demonstration of my inner spirit taking charge, the profound effect of this experience has stayed with me to this day. I wonder if this is what enlightenment really entails. Maybe it is not about learning and growing and evolving your personality self through much struggle and sacrifice. Maybe it is just a matter of surrendering your ego to the spirit within you. Maybe all you have to do is *let go*.

THINGS FALL APART

Chris, Peter, and I had been living together in a charming little house on Coronado Island near San Diego for a couple of months, our eventual move to Hawai'i a regular topic of discussion. On our latest visit to the Big Island, we had looked at a property in south Puna near the ocean, which included the cement frame of an unfinished home. We traipsed about the lush green land, fantasizing about our new life there.

"I could have a charming little cottage right here," I said, standing in an open meadow. Peter, an interior decorator by trade, was already imagining the finished house, his large blue eyes dreamy and glazed over.

Chris sprinted up the stairs. "Our bedroom will have an ocean view," he exclaimed to Peter with delight.

We picked out the perfect place for our garden, rich with volcanic soil, and I buried some of the turquoise I had received from the shaman who'd visited my shop a couple years before. All this despite the fact that we did not have the means to purchase the land, but we all believed that if it was meant for us to live in Hawai'i, Spirit would find a way to get us there.

* * * * *

In spite of our plans and dreams about Hawai'i, all did not bode well in the Coronado house. Emotions ran high as we each pushed one another's buttons. Peter liked the house immaculate, a concept that did not compute with Chris and me. Chris wanted a partner who was always open and loving and demonstrative, while Peter vacillated between warm and open to cold and distant. Peter liked to think out loud and did not necessarily do everything he said. Chris and I verbalized only what we meant to follow through on, and were exasperated when Peter would say one thing, then do something else or nothing at all. Chris wanted us to have meals together, but dinner could be set on the table and Peter would put on his jogging shoes to go for a run, leaving Chris and me feeling hurt and angry.

One evening, Peter and I were having dinner at a restaurant near the Light Spot while Chris was working with a client.

"Well, I guess this relationship is not going to make it," Peter said.

I dropped the menu. "What do you mean? We have plans to move to Hawai'i, don't we?" A pang of anxiety stabbed at my chest.

Peter was silent for a moment, avoiding my horrified gaze. He placed the menu on the table and explained: "When we first got together, Chris seemed like a fun-loving, easy-going, happy sort of guy. But now I see that he's not like that most of the time. He's always complaining about one thing or the other. He's rarely happy or fun anymore."

The waiter arrived to take our orders. I pushed Peter's comments to the back of my mind, unwilling even to entertain the idea that Chris and Peter might break up.

* * * * *

A few weeks later, I waited at the airport gate to meet Chris. He had been in San Francisco for a week performing in a men's choir. He spotted me first, sauntering forth and enveloping me in a warm hug.

"This is my friend Patti," he said, introducing me to another man. He was about six feet tall with fair hair and an honest, wholesome-looking face. "This is Ryan."

I shook Ryan's hand.

"You wait here, sweetie," Chris said, patting Ryan on the back. "I'll get the luggage."

Sweetie? I narrowed my eyes, scrutinizing Ryan from head to toe. *What's going on?*

The three of us piled into my car. Chris gave me directions to Ryan's apartment. I thought we were just dropping him off and gawked in disbelief when he pulled his own luggage out of the car, along with Ryan's.

"What are you doing?" I asked. My dreams of moving to Hawai'i with my two best friends had just crumbled down around me.

"I'm staying with Ryan tonight. I'll explain later. Don't say anything to Peter."

"But…"

"I'll be back tomorrow and explain everything," he said, kissing me on the cheek. He grabbed his suitcase and hurried after Ryan.

I drove home, my stomach in knots. How could he do this? We were all going to Hawai'i. We were going to buy property together. How could this have happened? And how was I going to confront Peter? He would surely know something was up when I came home without Chris.

Truth be told, their relationship hadn't been going very well in recent months. There were arguments. Disagreements. I recalled a bitter fight several weeks before. I could hear their loud voices from my bedroom, but I had no idea what the argument was about. Suddenly, Chris stormed out of their bedroom clutching a white teddy bear Peter had given me as a gift. "You think he's so nice and kind and generous, do you?" he screamed, shoving the teddy bear in my face. "He didn't even buy this for you." His voice rose an octave. "*I* bought it! I pointed it out to him at the store and told him that you'd like it. He picked it up, but when we got to the check out counter, he didn't have enough money on him, so I paid for it. He gives it to you, takes the credit, and never pays me back. Go ask him if you don't believe me!"

What the hell?

"Go ahead! Ask him!"

I slunk into their bedroom, teddy bear in tow. Peter stared at me incredulously when I asked the question. He finally admitted that he didn't remember the details. He thought he'd paid Chris back.

Recalling that senseless argument made my stomach churn. I didn't want to face Peter now. *Maybe he'll be out jogging. Maybe he went to the gym…*

But as soon as I got home, Peter cornered me in the kitchen.

"Where's Chris?"

"Ah, he's not here."

His forehead furrowed. "He didn't come back?

"Well…"

"Tell me the truth, Patti. What happened? Did he meet someone?" His face was drawn and pinched.

I tried to resist, but he dragged the information out of me.

"I knew it. I could feel it!" He put on his jogging shoes and charged out of the house, slamming the door. I curled up under my blanket. What was going to happen now? I felt bad for Peter; confused about Chris. And what about Hawai'i?

Chris returned the following day and moved into the living room. He explained to me that he had fallen in love with Ryan. A knot constricted my throat. Peter and Chris had been together a little more than a year. How can a person fall in and out of love so quickly? True, I had loved Bahman and later separated from him, but that was after fifteen years of marriage, after I had grown and changed and evolved to the point that we had little left in common. Maybe I just didn't understand gay men.

With a knotted stomach and aching heart, I watched things go downhill from there. Chris and Peter hardly spoke to each other anymore. The energy in the house went from bad to worse.

There were a few arguments, although for the most part they ignored one another. Nerves were raw and stretched. Anger. Disappointment. Disillusionment. These were the energies that hung in the air, like hungry spirits ready to suck out our very souls.

In the fall, Ryan's company transferred him to San Francisco. Chris packed up and moved with him. I was left running The Inner Visions Center and living with Peter. I was lost, furious, confused. I had left my husband and lost my best friend and felt completely and utterly abandoned.

What is happening? I asked my spirit.

You will be in Hawai'i in three months, chimed the voice. *You have nothing to fear.*

Three months? With no friends. No support. My pulse roared in my ears. *Why?*

Be at peace and trust, said the voice.

Easy for Spirit to say: it was my life in shambles. Nevertheless, deep down, I had the feeling that my spirit spoke true.

I recalled a session I had attended a couple of years earlier with Louise Hay, now a famous author and teacher. In her sixties, she was vibrant, serene, loving. I sat on the floor with about thirty other people, many of them young men dying of AIDS. We held hands and sang a soothing song called *Doors Closing, Doors Opening,* a song about accepting change and knowing that we were safe. I remembered the initial tension in the room, the sadness, the tears. I remembered holding hands and swaying softly, chanting and singing the song, over and over. I remembered the sense of release, of comfort, of love and acceptance.

Wanting, no, *needing* to recapture that feeling while there was so much tumult in the Coronado house, I bought the tape with that song and played it over and over again, singing along with the tune, taking it to heart. I sang it in the car, in the shower, in the Light Spot, while taking long walks in Balboa Park or around Coronado Island. The song soothed me as I struggled to deal with the upheaval with Chris and Peter, the pain of losing my friends, and the fear of having to begin a new life all alone. I was going to have to let go of everything and everyone and move on and this terrified me.

In spite of my fears, I knew deep down that this was something I had to do, needed to do. The island was calling to me, reaching out to me, tugging at my heart. I rationalized that my longing for Hawai`i was because of the warm weather; even San Diego had chilly winter nights. Or it was because of the small size of Hilo; the traffic in San Diego was getting hectic. Or perhaps I just needed change. But in reality, it was none of these things. My spirit was directing me to move to Hawai`i, a land with the energy I needed to help me grow; a place where there were people I had to meet and challenges I had to face, catalysts that would provide me with the tools and impetus I needed to grow and change and evolve.

On one of our trips to Hilo, I had applied for a teaching position at the university. I was told that they had no openings, but they would keep my resume on file should anything come up.

In the summer of 1989, the university contacted me for an interview for a full-time position as an English as a Second Language instructor. I flew over, conducted the interview, then returned to San Diego and waited and waited and waited. Over two months passed with no word.

My stomach clenched as I dialed the number. "No word yet," the program director said. "But you can come and teach a couple of reading classes as a lecturer this semester."

"No, I'll wait for the position," I replied. I refused to move to Hawai'i, only to find out that the position had been given to someone else and I would be left with a part time job and no benefits.

I hung up, shaking, my stomach clenched. Leaving my husband, friends, family, job, and business and moving to Hawai'i required a major leap of faith. It felt like jumping into a void with nothing to hold on to.

Raising my hands to the heavens, tears streaking down my face, my body shaking, I cried out to God, "If you want me to move to Hawai'i, I will do it, but I need to get this job. I need to have at least some stability. This is my request."

After this declaration, I felt oddly calm and at peace.

Several days later, the phone rang.

"Are you ready to move to Hawai'i?" said the program director.

"I, ah...I think so."

"Okay, we're waiting for you. You got the job."

I paused, hardly believing my ears.

"The job starts January first. See you soon."

I hung up the phone and fell back in my chair, staring blankly into the bustling traffic outside the Light Spot door.

I'm really moving to Hawai'i.

I later learned that the position had initially been offered to another applicant, but he had turned down the job because the university was unwilling to pay for his relocation costs. I had been their second choice.

The universe had opened the door.

* * * * *

Now that I had the job, my separation from Bahman had become real. With heavy hearts, Bahman and I signed the divorce papers and I filed them with the county.

I was 39 and single and beginning a new life.

Our Contracts

Many cultures and religions define "marriage" as two people vowing to stick together through thick and thin until "death do us part." Yet, are these really God's conventions? Or, like everything else in this world, does it vary depending on the individuals involved and their real purpose and reason for being together?

Before we are born, I believe that our souls make sacred contracts with other souls. These sacred contracts include the potential to meet and form relationships so that we can assist one another to awaken to who we are and fulfill our life's purpose. These relationships may be kinship, romantic, friendship, business, or casual acquaintance. Some may even be antagonistic. These potential relationships may be short term or life long, yet they will all have one thing in common: to propel us forward in our spiritual development and our higher purpose in life.

Imagine the plot of a good book, a play, or movie. The story usually includes a main character who, after facing challenges, learns, grows, and is finally transformed. In order for the plot to work, the main character needs an antagonist, either in the form of a person, an institution, a difficult situation, or a natural disaster. In most cases, other actors have to play the role of the antagonist in order for the story to work. A significant fact to remember, especially when dealing with other people who could be just playing their agreed-upon roles.

When faced with the hardships and the difficult choices, the main character is forced to tap into an inner strength and capabilities that he would never have needed or even known he possessed without the conflict or challenge. This is the "hero's path," as Joseph Campbell calls it. The path we must all take in order to evolve.

While many call these challenges "lessons," I prefer to call them "training sessions," since the word "lesson" can also have a negative connotation. In other words, we have accepted a mission, we have come to earth with a purpose, and, like any job, we need training in order to acquire the skills necessary to get the job done. The "training sessions" of life help us develop and hone these skills. It is the challenges of life that transform us.

Why did I have to separate from my husband in order to continue on my spiritual journey? Did Bahman's soul have a contract to love and support me until I reached a level of growth necessary to take the next step? Had our patterns with one another run their course so that we no longer felt a draw, need, or desire to be together? Had our souls fulfilled their contracts? I wasn't sure, but believing this as a possibility helped me deal with the emotional wrench of separating from him.

Life in Hawai'i

In January, 1990, I moved to the Big Island of Hawai'i. Peter had been vacationing there with a friend over Christmas. He greeted me at the airport and helped me find temporary housing with a mutual friend. Peter also agreed to look for a place for me to live while I was at work during the day. After spending years in cramped apartments, I was unwilling to settle for anything less than a house, even if I had to commute.

A few days after I'd started my new job, Peter picked me up after work. "I found you a house," he said, blue eyes dancing. "I think you'll like it."

Twenty minutes later, I stepped into a three-bedroom house with cedar wood walls, a spacious living, dining and kitchen area, and a reasonable rent. I loved the large, open feeling, the high ceilings, the warmth of wood walls. I especially loved the bedroom upstairs with its hardwood floor. Two extra bedrooms provided elbow room and a place for house guests. Just a twenty minute drive to the university and only $425 a month.

"I'll take it!" I exclaimed with delight.

* * * * *

Peter had said his goodbyes and left several days before, promising to come back and visit me soon. I kneeled on the shaggy orange carpet of my house, hugging the white teddy bear he had given me. Here I was, in a place that might as well be another planet, where I knew no one and hardly understood the cultural norms. For the first time in my life, I was completely alone. Tears wetted my cheeks. *What have I done?*

All will be well, said my inner voice with a soothing tone. *Fear not. All will be well.*

Bolstered by my inner voice, I pulled myself together. I decided to focus on what I want my new life to look like rather than moping around feeling sorry for myself. I went to town and purchased what I needed to create new treasure maps.

That weekend, I kneeled amid piles of magazines strewn about the floor, cutting out pictures and pasting them onto cardboard posters while large teardrops fell. Regardless of my feelings of loneliness and fear, I was determined to use all the tools in my power to create the life I wanted. I flipped through magazines and cut out pictures of loving relationships, healthy, vibrant women, pictures of homes, inside and out, an array of healthy foods: grains, vegetables, and fruits, photos of friends having fun together, exotic places to travel, herbs and herbal medicines, a subject I wanted to learn more about, pictures demonstrating financial comfort and ease, and photos of people enjoying and loving life… Out of these many pictures I created a collage, adding words and phrases and affirmations with bright color markers. I stood back, arms folded, examining my handiwork with satisfaction. An entire wall of my living room was now decorated with a row of treasure maps—pictures and phrases showing my every want, my every dream, my every desire, especially the soulmate I was supposed to meet depicted by a happy couple, laughing with one another. The man was tall with dark hair graying at the sides.

I wiped my tears and smiled with satisfaction.

THE FEMININE PRINCIPLE

My work did not stop with the treasure maps. I participated in a self-empowerment workshop offered at the local Church of Religious Science. After the weekend was over, my working group, all women, began meeting once a week.

Other than a couple of high school friends, I had had little companionship with women over the course of my life, although I can't say exactly why. Maybe I didn't want to repeat my mother's life, stuck for years in the house with four small kids and no life; maybe I found talk of babies and cooking and fashion, main topics of discussion among Iranian women of the 1960s, too boring for words; maybe I wrote women off after my mother left me. Whatever the reason, I was simply not comfortable getting close to women.

Meeting with and making friends with women was a new and welcome experience. We shared our lives, our problems, our challenges, and our goals. We listened to each other. Supported each other. Encouraged each other. My friendships with Bahman, Chris, and Peter had mostly revolved around *doing* – we had coffee, ate out at numerous restaurants, watched a video or a TV program, combed the mall or specialty shops for a particular item that was just right, went to the movies, or took trips together. My interactions with women had an entirely different flavor. The emphasis was on *being* with one another, regardless of location or activity. We shared our feelings: our loves, our fears, our hopes, our dreams. I told them of the psychic's prediction and my own visions of a new man coming into my life. I shared my fears and anxieties about this, wondering where he was and why he hadn't shown up yet. I allowed them to coach and console me. "It will happen," they said. "Be patient, it will happen." As the months passed, I became more and more comfortable in the company of women and called a number of them my friends.

Gaining courage, support, and momentum, I began exploring other women's groups: *Support groups* where women were given time to talk about their issues and problems and received support and encouragement from the others; *Wise Women groups,* consisting of women 40 and up, discussing issues about body image and aging and relationships; *Full Moon Circles* where we sat around an open fire on white plastic chairs while a leader guided us into meditation. We all thirsted for the love and support of other women, something sadly missing in our culture.

Yet these groups had only whetted my palate. Ed had given me a few books about Celtic earth-based religions and suggested I read *The Mists of Avalon* by Marianne Zimmer Bradley. Fascinated, I craved to know more, to go deeper, to explore the mystery of the feminine. Plunging into numerous books on women's spirituality and earth-based religions, especially pre-Christian European traditions, opened my eyes to a brave new world. I read books on Goddess Spirituality, Wicca, Druidism, Pagan and Neo-Pagan belief systems. Old images of green-faced witches with crooked noses casting evil spells and eating children's souls gave way to pictures of women as midwives, herbal healers, wise counselors and shamans: people following a path of personal responsibility and individual spiritual growth in harmony with the earth and all of life, acknowledging the cycles of nature and the divinity in all things.

While none of these traditions is based on doctrine or dogma, I discovered many similar ideas and concepts across the spectrum: If it harms none, do what you will; live in balance and harmony with nature; take personal responsibility for your actions and deeds; understand that life is cyclic and your immortal soul does not end with the physical death of your body; foster free thought and will of the individual and encourage self-discovery; know that whatever you give out in thought, words, or actions, comes back to you three times fold; acknowledge the equality of all people and the right of each individual to follow his or her own way to spiritual enlightenment.

Modern neo-pagans see the divine as both imminent and transcendent, that which is manifest to our awareness and that which is not. In other words, the spirit of the one exists in all things and manifests itself in feminine and masculine aspects, God and Goddess, each with unique characteristics resulting in a harmonious creation of life. *The many faces of the one…*

This concept of the feminine aspect of divinity is not limited to Pagan beliefs. In Hinduism it is called Shakti, in Judaism, Hochna, or its Greek translation, Sophia, in Christianity, the Holy Spirit or Holy Ghost, although some Christian sects do not view it as such.

Could it be that many of the problems of the world stemmed from our lopsided view of divinity? From our lack of honor and acknowledgement of the feminine aspect within our own beings, regardless of gender? Would things change, would *we* change, if we acknowledged and honored the Feminine Principle of divinity both in the world and within our own hearts?

Now that I had gained a basic understanding of these spiritual systems, I thirsted for the *experience,* and came together with a group of women. We decided to have monthly gatherings to empower ourselves, to support one another, and to honor and acknowledge the Goddess within us all.

* * * * *

The harvest moon looms large and bright in the night sky. The fire hisses and crackles, flames reaching up like fingers of light to dispel the darkness. We sit in a circle; faces lit softly, the evening air moist on our skin. The beat of the drum rises into the night, in tune with the thumping of our hearts. The leader tosses herbs into the fire, the musky fragrance heightening our senses. Our minds quiet, our thoughts, worries, and concerns dissipate as we sway to the beat of the drum, in the light of the fire, under the open sky.

The leader begins to chant about weaving our own reality.

Slowly we begin to chant along, voices joining together, rising, surging…pulses quickening.

"I let go of anger," says one woman, symbolically throwing her anger into the fire. We continue the chant. The drum beats louder.

"I release victimhood," cries another, hurling it into the flames. Our voices rise an octave, acknowledging her.

"I let go of shame," says a third, casting it away from her with both hands. Her face brightens.

The chanting rises, reaching a crescendo. The drum beats, faster and faster.

"I release feelings of *not enough*," I howl. The moon looks down on me as if smiling.

We cast away many more negative feelings, doubts and fears, allowing them to be burned and purified by the flames. A cool breeze blows wisps of our hair.

We rise, singing in one voice, woman's voice, floating around the fire, swaying, dancing to the beat of the drum and the song of our hearts. Arms and legs move as if they have been freed from lifelong imprisonment, swirling, swaying, gyrating... We drop to the soft grass panting, giggling like children.

I wrap my sweater around me for warmth, lie down on a blanket, and close my eyes as the leader guides us into a shamanic journey with a soft, slow beat of the drum. I see myself walking through a magical forest, the black jaguar, my spirit guide, padding by my side. I step inside the opening of a large tree and descend a spiral stairway lit by torches. Jaguar walks a few steps ahead, assuring me it is safe. Down and down we go, the only sound our soft footsteps and the beating of my heart.

We reach a landing and emerge onto a forest path with brilliant green trees, flitting butterflies, and small animals peeking out of the brush. We come upon a clear water spring. Reposing gracefully on a boulder is the Goddess Brigid with flaming red hair, sparkling green eyes, and a sheer, cascading, blue gown. "I have been waiting for you to call on me," she says, folding me in a motherly embrace.

I recall that I am supposed to bring an offering. "I offer to do a service for humanity," I stammer, "but I'm not sure I am up to the task."

Brigid's emerald eyes sparkle. She grabs me and peels off my outer form, layer by layer, until she reaches my inner core – a being of pure light. "Remember who you are," she says with a smile. She gives me a gift: an oval-shaped mirror.

"Whenever you look in this mirror, you will see your true self," she adds.

The drum beats faster, signaling the time for return. Jaguar nudges me. He has grown larger. He directs me to climb on his back. I bow my head in honor of the Goddess, take my leave, and hold on tight to black jaguar as he leaps through the forest, up the stairs, and out of the tree.

We slowly awaken, some sitting, some lying down, faces radiant and serene, and share our experiences in seeking the Goddess within and the wisdom she has shared.

We retreat to the house and share healthy, life-giving food. We chat and we laugh and we revel in one another's company. One woman volunteers to lead the next group at her place. We hug warmly and depart. I drive home under the light of the moon, feeling buoyant, invigorated, and fulfilled.

* * * * *

The following year, Chris moved to the Big Island, while Ryan stayed in San Francisco and agreed to come and visit regularly. Chris had visited me in Hawai'i a number of times and I had let go of my anger with him, realizing that he had needed to follow his heart. I was happy that Chris had finally come. He was still my best friend and I loved him dearly, but things were different now. The dynamics of our relationship had changed. I had made a life for myself apart from my family, apart from Bahman, apart from Chris, apart from Peter. I was coming into my own.

One afternoon, Chris and I sat on the couch in my house sipping lemon-flavored sparkling water. I was trying to make him understand my new experiences and beliefs in feminine spirituality. I got up and stood in front of him, gesturing for emphasis. "It's not much different than Religious Science."

Chris crossed his long legs, a confused look on his face.

"What do you do when you perform a Spiritual Mind Treatment? You declare your *intent,* focus on what you want, accept it is so, and release it to Spirit. Right?"

He nodded, not sure where this was going.

"All right. Now, instead of a Spiritual Mind Treatment, or creative visualization, or writing or saying affirmations, you do a ritual. You focus your mind on the desired result and create a ritual or ceremony around it with candle, incense, drum or rattle. Your intent can be made into a rhyme that you repeat over and over, like a song or a chant. It's just a way of focusing your attention, involving all the senses. It's really no different!"

His face told me that he was not buying this.

"Did you think that Ernest Holmes was the first person to discover that thought creates form? That we have the power within us to change our lives? This is not *new* information. It's been known by the shamans and mystics all over the world for hundreds, maybe even thousands of years. It's called *magic*. The Church of Religious Science just put it into a format with a minister and Sunday church service palatable to the Western mind set."

Chris nodded, but the look in his eyes told me that this was too much to digest, at least at the moment. I let it go at that.

I thought about how the medieval church had dissuaded people from taking control of their own lives, spinning our God-given power of creativity into something evil, portraying herbalists, healers, midwives, shamans, and strong, independent European women as "those consorting with the devil," an entity the so-called "witches" didn't even believe in, much less consort with. I wondered if the church had believed in what it was doing or if they intentionally wanted people to stay ignorant and in the dark.

Terry Cole-Whittaker once said that Jesus's comment "the meek will inherit the earth" does not refer to the victims, the pushovers, the sheep of the world. She doesn't believe in victims. "*Meek* means those still open and able to learn. Be ye as little children to enter the kingdom of God." Children, who still have the sense of awe, of wonder. Children, who are open to new things, new ideas. Children, who are willing to learn, to explore, to expand. Children, who can still see the mystery and believe in the magic.

As I hugged Chris goodbye that afternoon at my house, I realized that our relationship had changed. We were now on divergent paths. Religious Science had been a step on my spiritual path, but for Chris, it was a place where he was comfortable and fulfilled. Maybe the patterns that had drawn us together had run their course. Maybe the contract of our souls had been fulfilled. Yet even though we no longer spent as much time together as before, we remained good friends.

THE SACRED HULA DANCE

"It should be fun." Chris had discovered a free hula class in Pahoa and couldn't wait to go. "Let's try it out. Tuesday night."

"I'm not really into dance," I said, resisting any form of physical activity as usual.

"Come on! How do you know? Maybe you'll love it."

"I guess…"

I purchased a few books on the subject and learned that the Hawaiian spiritual tradition known as *Huna,* which hula is a part, is ancient, its teachings passed down orally from generation to generation. A system of personal development and spiritual discipline, it teaches its adherents balance, respect for the land, and ways to increase one's life force energy or *mana*. The chants, *meles,* and the movements, *hula,* are integrated parts of this shamanistic spiritual system. In other words, hula is not a mere dance as I had originally thought. Hula is prayer in motion.

Though Chris dropped out after the first two sessions, I took part in classes on a regular basis in ancient hula (*hula kahiko*), modern hula (*hula a'uana*), and chant (*mele*). I was particularly fond of the ancient hula class. Wrists and ankles adorned with ti leaf leis, our hips swayed, feet pounded, and voices chanted to the beat of the gourd, creating an energy and vibration that was palpable. I didn't realize it at first, but the motions, specifically the movement of the hips, was opening blockages in my spine and releasing life force energy or *mana.*

Over the course of a year, I became slimmer, stronger, more energetic, and physically fit. And while I attempted to intellectually learn more about the spiritual path of Huna, the teacher, or *kumu,* was unwilling to provide any additional information. Maybe he thought I wasn't ready. Maybe he just didn't want to teach me. Available books on the subject did not intrigue me, and no other teacher appeared.

In the fall of 1991, my class was graduating from the first level of hula. The graduation included a hula and chant to Pele, the volcano Goddess, performed on a special platform set aside for this purpose in Hawai`i Volcanoes National Park. Preparation for the graduation was elaborate. We spent hours practicing the chant and the movements, created geometric designs on our costumes with sticks and colored dyes, harvested plants and created leaf leis for our heads, neck, wrists and ankles (no flowers are used in ancient hula). We put our wet hair in tiny braids overnight so it flowed down our backs in small curls the next morning. We picked fragrant leaves and placed them between the folds of our costumes, then reverently carried them with us for the ritual hula at the park.

In a small grass shack near the hula platform, we buzzed about like bees in a hive, preparing for the occasion. Dressed and decked with leaf leis, we lined up, hands held at chest level, elbows straight out, fingers facing each other in the proper pose, and silently strode towards the platform.

A few friends and family members sat on the grass to watch, but this was not a performance. It was a sacred ritual. The kumu hula and other drummers sat to one side of the platform with their backs to the audience. We took our positions on the grass-covered platform. A moment of silence stretched as a cardinal flitted among the o'hia trees.

The kumu beat the gourd and the leader began the chant. We chanted in unison, feet pounding to the beat of the gourd, hand movements telling the story of Pele, fire Goddess of the volcano. In the distance, the steam from Kileaua crater, Pele's home, rose to the heavens.

A final beat of the gourd and the dance ended. We stood straight with serious faces (smiling is not appropriate in ancient hula.) Turning, we silently walked off the stage in a queue. According to the kumu, we had only graduated from kindergarten to first grade. We were now serious hula dancers and our real work had just begun. Nevertheless, my intuitive guidance told me that I had learned what I needed to learn; that the movements, the chants, and the sacred graduation ceremony had connected me to this land and its traditional culture, but more importantly, the hula had freed stuck energies within my body.

My work with hula was complete.

Meeting My Soulmate

I had been living on the island of Hawai'i for one year and nine months, but my soulmate was no where in sight. Part of me was anxious and confused over this, yet another part loved the freedom, the growth, the opportunity to make my own choices, walk my own path, and discover who I really was inside. Little by little, I was peeling away the old layers of limitation and judgment, allowing the real me to shine through. I was finally feeling good about myself, happy with who I was.

On a bright Sunday morning, just two weeks after I had graduated from my hula class, I woke up with visions of Hawai'i Volcanoes National Park dancing through my head. "It's a nice day for a hike," I thought and called an acquaintance who enjoyed hiking.

In the parking lot at the trail head, I noticed Sue, a woman from hula class, and her boyfriend Charlie, whom I had previously met, sitting on the bed of a truck putting on their socks and hiking shoes. A second man, whom I had never met, stood nearby.

I strode up to greet them.

"This is my friend, Mark," Charlie said, gesturing to the other man. "He just arrived from Boston."

Mark was tall, about a foot taller than me. He wore dark glasses. I couldn't see his eyes.

"Nice to meet you." He extended one hand.

Just as I clasped his hand, an electric current coursed through my body giving me a mild shock. I glanced up at him and noticed pitch black hair feathering to white on the sides, a sign I was directed to look for when I met my soulmate. I let go of his hand and stumbled back a step.

Stunned, I stared at him with dinner plate eyes as my friend chatted with Charlie and Sue. Afterwards, Mark, Sue, and Charlie headed down one trail, and we took another as we'd planned. I spent the next few hours talking nonstop with my hiking partner as if I needed to fill in the empty air between us and distract myself from the encounter.

Later that afternoon, my hiking partner dropped me off at my house. I turned the key in the lock and stepped through the door and a flood of energy washed over me.

Contact this man, said my inner voice, not in the usual whisper, but more like a voice booming through my head. Energy swept up and down my body in waves. *This is the person you are meant to meet,* said the voice again.

I paced back and forth in the room, scrambling to get my bearings as my palms sweat, my stomach churned, and the hairs on my arms stood on end. *Could this be it? Could this be my soulmate, the person I've been looking for? Waiting for? Longing for?*

YES! My inner spirit replied.

I collapsed on the couch and cried.

An hour passed before I was able to pull myself together and work up the courage to call Sue.

* * * * *

"Well, you need to know that he's not the kind of guy who dates women casually," she said. "He likes to get to know them first."

"Works for me." I agreed. "We can all get together. How about next weekend?"

Sue paused. I played with the telephone cord. "Well, I'm going to be pretty busy the next couple of weeks with work. How about three weeks from now?"

"Three weeks!"

"Sorry, but that's the best I can do."

"Okay. See you then." I put the phone down and wiped sweat from my forehead. *Three weeks!*

Those three weeks were the longest weeks I can ever remember. A jumble of mixed emotions, I was barely able to contain myself, believing I'd never make it through. I wracked my brain, trying to remember what Mark looked like. Our meeting had lasted no more than a few minutes and he'd been wearing dark glasses. I marked off each day on my calendar with a big black X until the day of our outing finally arrived.

* * * * *

I stole quick, furtive glances to try and get a better idea of his features before we entered the darkness of the lava tubes. *Are those green eyes?* He seemed to be even shier than I was, averting his gaze.

Mark and I followed Sue and Charlie into caves made from lava rock, using flashlights to light our way. Some sections had wide open chambers, other areas were narrow. At one point we had to walk like ducks to get past a low-ceilinged area. *What a strange place to choose for a first outing,* I thought. *I can't even see the man!*

Near the end of the lava tube, we took a break and rested on large rocks. Mark talked about beginning a new life in Hawai'i and wondered whether he was going to make it financially.

He'll do well, said my inner voice, loud and clear. I was surprised to hear this since I rarely got information about other people. "You'll do well in Hawai'i," I told him, although I couldn't make him out in the darkness. "Trust me. You'll do well."

"I hope so," he said.

A couple weeks later, there was a dinner party at Sue's house. The following week, another one at mine. During these dinners, we talked of inconsequential things: the weather, Sue's artwork, her beautiful house, the food, and the fact that Mark had been on the island for only 11 days when we met at the park. At this point, he felt comfortable enough to meet me alone. He called a few days later and said he'd drop by the house after work.

That evening, I nervously paced back and forth in the living room, shaking out my hands as if the tension would fly off like drops of water. My stomach felt like lead. Sweat dripped down the side of my face. *Forty years old and you'd think I was a teenager going on my first date!* I tried to calm myself through rationalization. It didn't work.

A car pulled into the driveway. I peeked through the Venetian blinds and noticed the large, round lights of his silver jeep. I smoothed my dress, dabbed sweat from my forehead, took a deep breath, and opened the door. My heart was beating so fast I was afraid he'd be able to hear it.

He stepped into the kitchen, tall and lithe with raven hair and deep Irish green eyes that sloped gently down on the sides. Thick Sean Conrey eyebrows and long lashes dramatized his eyes. Kind eyes. A gentle face. In a crowd, he'd be the one you'd turn to, the one you'd feel comfortable asking for help. He was simply dressed in a plain T-shirt and faded jeans. No pretensions. No need to impress me. He was just being himself.

"Hi, Patti," he said with a smile and embraced me in a gentle hug. Suddenly, all the tension released from my body in one big swoop. My heartbeat came back to normal, like I had hugged a grounding rod that took all my scattered, nervous energy and pulled everything back into balance and harmony. I stood back and looked at him with wide eyes. No more sweat. No more tension. Just peace.

We sat in the living room on a futon couch and chatted over tea while my newly adopted kitten, Precious, played in our laps. I noticed his hands. Soft, gentle hands with long fingers. Creative hands. The kind that painted or sketched or played the piano.

"I'm actually from Burlington," he said, "It's a small town north of Boston."

"I was born in Lowell."

"Lowell, Massachusetts?" He raised one eyebrow.

"Yeah, but I don't remember much. Only lived there for a few years before we moved to New Jersey and later Ohio. How far is Lowell from Burlington?"

"It's just a few towns over; 20, 25 miles, maybe."

"Fancy meeting you all the way over here," I said. We both chuckled.

Precious, my grey and white kitten with a stub for a tail, started to claw at Mark's crotch. Heat rose to my face. "Precious, stop that!" I said, reaching to remove the precocious animal. "You'll ruin Mark's pants."

"He's okay," Mark said, tenderly petting the kitten's head. "They're just old dungarees." Precious calmed down, curled up on Mark's lap, and purred.

"Dungarees?"

"What do you call them?"

"Jeans."

Precious was fast asleep when Mark rose to leave. He softly placed the kitten on the couch, attempting not to wake him.

Mark was of the old school, as far as relationships were concerned. He had great respect for women and pursued a relationship slowly and with great care, much like old-fashioned courtship. It was important for him to get to know the woman well before he took things any further, unusual for a man in the '90s. A part of me admired this in a man. Another part of me was screaming to get things moving. And while I had clear guidance that this was the man I was meant to be with, he was not so sure. As a result, he took things slowly, visiting my house every couple of weeks.

* * * * *

It was about two months after we'd first met. I took a deep breath as his jeep barreled up the driveway about half an hour late.

"Sorry I'm late," he said. "Something's wrong with my vehicle. I'll have to take it in tomorrow."

I poured two cups of tea. At the time, I didn't know that he disliked tea; he was too polite to tell me. He would have preferred a cup of coffee.

"You have artist hands," I said, admiring the long, gentle fingers. "Do you play the piano?"

Mark leaned back on the futon couch, long legs crossed. "No, but I do like to draw and sometimes paint. I'll show you some of my artwork next time I come over."

I blew on my cup and took a sip of tea. "Have you ever been married?"

"Never met the right woman. And you?"

"I was married for fifteen years. Things didn't work out."

He nodded and played with Precious. "Did you ever want children?"

"Maybe, when I was younger, but I'm over it. I can't have them now."

A broad smile spread across his face. "I never wanted children," he said. "They're a great responsibility. If I had children, I'd want to give them my all, but there are so many other things I want to do in my life. I like to travel, for example. I've been to most parts of the country."

No children. Loves to travel. Yes! Bahman hadn't liked traveling much. I'd had to drag him to the few places we did visit. He'd never wanted to drive very far.

On his next visit, Mark shared his artwork: pencil drawings of flowers and birds in exquisite detail. "These are pretty good," I said. "Have you taken art classes?"

"No. Just learned from books."

We chatted away the evening. It felt *good* to be with Mark. Effortless. Comforting.

On his following visit, I asked about his spiritual beliefs.

"When I was younger, my father used to take my brother, my sister, and me to the Catholic Church."

"Your dad, not your mom?"

"My mom didn't go back then. So when I was fourteen, I told my father that I didn't want to go anymore. The sermons were always about our sins. I told Dad that I didn't think I was a sinner."

"What did he say?"

"Nothing. He said okay and stopped taking me. I guess he felt that he'd done his job of giving me some sense of religion."

Mark explained that in his twenties, he'd read a number of books on spirituality such as *Autobiography of a Yogi* by Yogananda and *The Mustard Seed* by Rajneesh. He concluded that we were all spiritual beings; that we didn't really need to *do* anything to be spiritual; that we didn't need to analyze every little thing about our life and try and figure it all out. Life was just the way it was. In his opinion, there was really nothing to do other than live our lives and be good people and enjoy the time we had.

It sounded like something Krishnamurti would say. *Maybe that works for Mark*, I thought, but for me, spiritual evolution involved doing and reading and experiencing and growing and trying to make sense of it all. Nevertheless, since Mark had a "live and let live" attitude, I sensed that our different spiritual approaches would not be an issue.

A few months after we'd met and become comfortable with one another, we went out on a few dates: A Chinese dinner, a Star Trek movie, a play at the university theatre. In late spring, Mark moved in, love blossomed, and I was barely touching the ground. I found myself smiling and laughing often and easily with this man. The more I got to know him, his kindness and generosity, the more I loved and admired him:

I mention that I need a new coffee table; the one I have is too small. A few days later, I come home from work and he is sawing away with wood and tools scattered all over the carport. "What are you doing?"

"Didn't you want a coffee table? I'm making you one," he replies matter-of-factly. By the weekend, our living room is furnished with a beautifully crafted and varnished oak coffee table, in addition to two end tables.

"Where did you learn to do that?" I inquire, examining the tables with admiration.

"I took a wood-working class in high school," he replies with a shrug.

* * * * *

I'm going out for a morning walk. It's a sunny day with only a few puffy clouds in the sky. About a mile away from the house, I'm caught in a downpour with no umbrella. I turn and begin walking back as fast as I can, cold and wet and miserable. Through the grey slate of rain, two round headlights appear. Mark pulls up his jeep and opens the door. I'm so touched by his thoughtfulness, I want to cry.

* * * * *

He brings me bouquets of flowers, greeting cards chosen with great care, or both. No reason. No special occasion. Just because. *Bahman never gave me flowers.*

* * * * *

While driving home from work, my car is rear-ended by a truck. I drag myself out of the car, shaken, my neck and back in pain. I'm explaining the incident to the policeman when Mark's silver jeep pulls up behind me. Surprised and relieved that he's magically appeared at my time of need, I melt into his warm embrace. He drives me to the hospital and stays by my side.

* * * * *

It's Christmas. We set up and decorate a tree. I get him a couple of gifts. On Christmas morning, I am stunned to find piles of gifts spread out under the tree: several books on healing and spirituality, a colorful backpack, a box of chocolates, a sweater for chilly nights, a stocking filled with incense and sweets, a teddy bear, a raincoat that folds up small and fits in a cover. And gifts from his family, sent from Massachusetts, although they've never met me: T-shirts, sweat shirts, mugs, a calendar of New England scenes. *Bahman never gave me this many gifts in our fifteen years of marriage.*

* * * * *

I'm stuck in the street with a flat tire. I walk to a pay phone and call Mark. He drops everything, drives into town, and changes the tire. A few days later, he gets us both cell phones. "So you can get a hold of me whenever you need me."

* * * * *

I'm in the living room, complaining about a teacher at work who's been giving me a hard time. I'm angry, tense. He listens for a few moments, stands up, and slides behind the sofa, crouching shorter and shorter, like he's descending into an imaginary basement. I stop my diatribe and chuckle. He stands up and makes a face: sad eyes, the corners of his mouth stretched all the way down like a painted clown. This hits my funny bone. I laugh so hard my eyes water, my sides ache. I forget all about the teacher at school.

* * * * *

I had opened myself up to love and experienced compassion with Chris and Peter and while holding the dying young man in my arms. But it was Mark who taught me the true meaning of love and compassion. His quiet, gentle love reached inside me and opened up the innermost petals of my heart—an intimacy I had craved for all my life.

My heart blossomed and I was euphoric, drunk with the ecstasy of loving and being loved by another human being, allowing myself to feel open, vulnerable, and soft.

And although I could sense loving feelings emanating from him, in truth, he was just creating a safe space for me to open the deepest chambers of my heart and allow the energy of love from my own spirit to flow forth. In other words, these euphoric feelings were coming from inside of me, not from without. Could this be the reason we are all so addicted to finding romantic love? Do we require someone to create a safe space that gives us permission to drop our guards and open our hearts so we can experience the unconditional love of God within our own beings? When we take on human form, we have the illusion of separation from source, from God. An inner longing to reconnect, to once again experience that feeling of oneness, propels us to look for something outside of ourselves to fulfill this need. I wonder if that drive to find and connect with our soulmate is, in truth, an outer manifestation of our deeper need to find God and reconnect with our spiritual selves.

They say that a good relationship takes work. That was not the case for us. Our relationship flowed like a gentle stream. He gave me the space to be myself and pursue my interests in spirituality, nutrition, herbal medicine, and writing: individually, in groups, at seminars, workshops, and conferences. I offered him the same courtesy in exchange as he focused on his passions: golf, art, photography, woodworking, collecting indigenous artwork, and landscaping. Ours was a quiet love, the type that started slowly and bore deeper as time passed. We enjoyed the simple things in life and looked forward to coming home each evening, our new kittens curled up on our laps as we watched a movie or a show on TV, or spent quiet reading time in bed, Mark with Clancy and Grisham and Koontz, I with books on spirituality, nutrition, writing, or literary and fantasy novels. We shared a passion for travel and a love of nature as we explored the island together and took trips to Alaska, Maui, and Kauai. And I knew, beyond a doubt, that this was the man I wanted to live with for the rest of my life.

When will we marry? I asked Spirit after a lengthy meditation.

Let go of all resentments and judgments of past relationships to allow love in, came the response.

I realized that I had cleared old patterns and learned to love and accept myself before I was able to attract a wonderful man like Mark into my life, so I was now determined to do whatever it took to deepen my relationship with him. I got a large yellow note pad and began writing down my anger, resentments, hurts and judgments about all the men who had touched my life—boyfriends, my first husband, teachers, authority figures, family members, the whole kit and caboodle. I visualized each person and addressed him directly, saying everything I had to say. Once all the negative feelings were out in the open, I said that I understood that each one had a role to play in my life, a contract to fulfill. I thanked them for fulfilling their contracts, forgave myself and forgave them, and released them from my psyche and my life.

After addressing every single male I could think of, I took the pad of yellow paper outside. Sitting cross-legged on the ground, I tore off the pages one by one, crumpled them up, and created a pile on the dirt driveway. Lighting a match, I set the pile of paper on fire and watched as the flames rose, licking the crumpled papers. Silent tears dripped out of the corners of my eyes as all my hurts and resentments went up in smoke.

When the papers had completely burned and the fire went out, I gathered the ashes and scattered them to the wind, then stretched out my arms and looked up into the evening sky feeling light, peaceful, and free.

Shortly thereafter, Mark proposed.

Chapter Ten: The Mystery of Synchronicity

There is no such thing as chance; and what seems to us merest accident springs from the deepest source of destiny.

– Friedrich Schiller

Syn.chro.nic.i.ty   Coincidence of events that seem to be meaningfully related, conceived in Jungian theory as an explanatory principle on the same order as causality.

-American Heritage Dictionary

Do coincidences shape our lives? Is there a magical force called synchronicity that nudges us toward our destiny and provides us with key information at just the right time?

The term "synchronicity" was coined by psychologist Carl Jung who had noted uncanny relationships between the content of his patients' dreams, odd coincidental events, and the restoration to mental health. According to Jung, synchronicity referred to "the acausal connecting principle" linking mind and matter—a connectedness that manifests itself through meaningful coincidences unexplainable by cause and effect.

Looking back at my own life, I find numerous examples of synchronous events that moved me in specific directions and shaped the course of my life.

When I was twenty-one and living in Iran, one of my first jobs was teaching English to kindergarten children in a private school. I taught the alphabet and numbers, nursery rhymes, and songs I remembered from my childhood, especially short tunes that included movements or gestures like "The Itsy Bitsy Spider," "The Little Teapot," and "Old MacDonald Had a Farm." The children learned the songs and gave dramatic performances at home to the delight and accolades of their parents. And while I enjoyed working with the children, the principal of the school was another matter.

One day, about mid-semester, I hustled down the corridor of the College of Literature and Foreign Languages to get to my evening English literature class. I was seething from a heated argument I'd had with the elementary school principal. He'd insisted that I fool the children into believing I didn't speak any Farsi; that I was an American and they were required to learn English in order to communicate with me. While I believed speaking to the children in English was a good idea, attempting to deceive a group of five-year-olds was an entirely different matter. *I need to look for another job,* I mumbled through gritted teeth as I reached the classroom door. *I just can't stand this man any longer.* I was running a little late and arrived just seconds ahead of the professor. Since my usual seat was already taken, I slipped into a spot in the front row next to an Air Force lieutenant, a man I had never met or noticed before.

As usual, I asked questions during the lesson and handled the assignment with ease. At the break, the officer chatted with me for a bit, wondering how I could speak English so well. After giving him a brief explanation, he said: "Well, why don't you come and teach at the Air Force Training Center? We're looking for new instructors."

I gulped. I didn't think I was even remotely qualified to teach Air Force cadets. "Well, ah…"

"You just have to take a test," he continued, placing his officer's hat on his head and rising to leave. "I'll bring the application next class." He shook my hand, said he was glad to make my acquaintance, and disappeared in the crowd of students milling in the hallway.

As promised, he brought me the application at the next class session, helped me fill it out, and delivered it to the appropriate office himself. I passed the test, completed their American-developed teacher training program, and began a new adventure as a civilian English instructor for the Imperial Iranian Air Force, a job that put me in contact with officers and cadets and foreign-educated Iranian teachers, in addition to a number of adventurous Americans—a brave new world of people, experiences, and ideas. My salary? Literally ten times what I had been getting from the private school.

On the evening I'd met the officer, another student had taken my usual seat. The space next to the officer was vacant, so I sat next to him. This happened exactly at the time I'd become fed up with my job and longed for a new one. On my own, I would have never even considered applying for a job at the Iranian Air Force. That new job changed the course of my life and it was there that I met my first husband, Bahman. Could this have been pure coincidence, or was the mysterious force of synchronicity at work?

*****

In 1975, I was twenty-four and teaching English as a Second Language in Tehran. My spiritual life had reached a standstill. After my experience with Hinduism, nothing further presented itself. I hungered for spiritual food, yet nothing in the area where I lived called to me. I was as thirsty as the dry, dusty desert of my environment. My environment had to change.

I stood in the break room at work, eyeing the colorful map of the United States on the wall. Bahman and I had discussed returning to the U.S. to continue our studies. *Where should we go?* I thought, scanning the vast expanse of states and cities. *So many choices.* My mother had passed away. My Uncle Ed had moved out west, no one knew where. I found no reason to return to New England—too cold. My grandmother was living in Florida with her retired navy husband, but Florida just didn't feel right.

Bahman had studied in the San Francisco Bay Area for several years and loved it. He believed California to be one of the most open-minded states in the U.S.—a hub of spirituality and new thought. *Hmmm…*

I found San Francisco on the map and checked its distance from the equator. *Still looks like it'd be cold.*

Putting my finger on the Bay City, I traced all the way down the California coast and stopped at the last major city before crossing the border to Mexico: San Diego.

I had never been to California and didn't know jack about the city of San Diego, but there was a "rightness" about it, a good feeling that washed over me like a pleasant spring rain. My finger tingled, as if a mild electric current were emanating from the map. *San Diego. And it should be warm that far south.*

"Are you coming to class, or are you going to just stand there fascinated with the land of your birth?" said a chubby male instructor who loved to tease everyone.

I turned and noticed that the other teachers had already left. Trooping after the portly tease, I smiled to myself. I *knew* I would be moving to San Diego. Knew it in my bones.

* * * * *

While I lived in San Diego and worked as a sales clerk to get myself through college, I was transferred to a new department after my hysterectomy. My new manager, Jared, convinced me to go to Terry Cole-Whittaker's church where I met my friend Chris in addition to many others on their spiritual path. This led me to explore the magical world of metaphysics, to open a bookstore and center, and expand my mind beyond my wildest dreams. And the decision to move to California did not affect only my and my husband's life: In 1979, my two sisters joined me in San Diego, went to college, married, had children, and live there to this day.

Could all of this have been mere coincidence or was there some mysterious guiding force with me the day of my decision, causing my finger to tingle when I touched San Diego on the map, making me feel good about moving there even though I knew nothing about the place?

Examining my life in more detail, I found numerous synchronous events:

1984—When I was depressed that Terry Cole-Whittaker was dissolving her church, the church program just *happened* to flip over on the car seat with Chris's name glaring up at me. By working with Chris, I'd let go of negative patterns and emotions I'd held onto since childhood.

1985—When I followed my intuitive guidance to open a bookstore and coffeehouse, the location appeared, within a matter of days, via one of Chris's clients. Running the Light Spot had been a marathon in mind expansion.

1991—When I followed a strong desire to hike through Volcanoes National Park one Sunday morning, I just *happened* to come across a friend from hula class with her boyfriend just minutes before they took off on their hike. And with them, my soulmate, the man with whom I would fall in love and marry.

READING THE PATTERNS

Did these events in my life happen by accident, coincidence, or luck, or was there some mysterious force in the universe, an ephemeral energy that connects all of life, all of creation, gently nudging me towards my destiny? If this mysterious force is what causes the *synchronicity* of events to take place, are we conscious participants in the process? Do we have to pay attention and follow the directions, the inner promptings, the *signs,* (like Mel Gibson in the movie *Signs*) for this synchronicity to take place?

God Outside the Box

In Hawai'i, I loved the waterfalls, the lush green landscape, and especially the rainbows. At times, I found myself worried about one thing or another, different scenarios running through my head. Whenever I saw a rainbow, my mind chatter would come to a dead stop, the tension in my muscles would release, and I'd grin like a kid on Christmas morning. To me, the rainbow was a message, a reminder that God was in charge and everything would be okay.

I had been living in Hawai'i for over a month when I went through a crisis of confidence. My immediate needs were easily met: a job, a decent car, an inexpensive rental home, yet I was feeling empty, as if a gaping hole had opened up in my gut that nothing could fill. I had no friends. No family. No bookstore with its streams of interesting and eccentric customers. No real spiritual food. No connection to anyone. On top of it all, Hilo was in one of those never-ending rainy patterns—dark and gray and wet. Doubt was spreading its ugly talons through my mind. Had I made the right decision? Was I really supposed to be here? Was it my destiny, part of my life plan? Or had I been influenced by Chris's enthusiasm and gone through with the plan even though Chris had apparently abandoned the idea and followed his new love to San Francisco?

I was driving to work that morning. The sky was a slate of gray. Huge raindrops attacked my windshield. *If I've made the right decision, give me a sign, God. I really need to be sure.*

Clouds separated and a shaft of light lit up the road in front of me. A magnificent rainbow stretched across the Hawaiian sky.

* * * * *

When I was living in San Diego and working at a department store, I was feeling low on energy although I was still in my twenties. I began to have thoughts of getting some form of physical exercise, unusual for me—physical activity had never been my "thing." At work, a middle-aged woman raved about the new gym she was going to and how working out there had increased her energy levels. After work that day, I stopped at the post office to pick up the mail. Before tossing my junk mail, I noticed an advertisement for an exercise machine that would do wonders to improve energy levels. Afterwards, on a whim, I took a different route home and passed by a towering billboard displaying a strong, healthy body. The message read: *Get fit!*

Getting the message loud and clear, I joined a gym.

* * * * *

About a year or so after we met, Mark told me about his own experience with signs:

"One night, a few months after we'd first met, I was sitting on a stone wall, alone, looking over Hilo Bay. Up to that point, we had not really gone *out* on a date—we were still getting to know one another."

I was all ears, wondering where this story was going.

"And while I was getting more comfortable with you, I still wasn't sure if you were the woman I was meant to be with. I thought about this for a while, watching the waves lap onto the lava rock. I needed to know; I needed to be sure. 'If Patti is the one for me,' I said out loud, 'show me a sign, God. Show me a sign in the next five minutes.'"

He paused, deep green eyes filled with love.

"Well, what happened?"

"Immediately after I said that, I looked up and saw a shooting star blaze across the sky. I took that as a sign that you were the right girl for me."

* * * * *

I had been a vegetarian for many years. So had Mark. I ate a healthy diet, or so I believed, ingested a slew of vitamins and herbs, and exercised regularly. In spite of all this effort, I was tired all the time. So tired, I could barely make it through the day. My weight went from plump to plain fat. My legs were stiff. My knees ached. At a loss, I sought help.

A naturopathic doctor suggested I add fish to my diet. "Oh, no," I replied, feeling justified in my dietary choice.

Two weeks later, I was working with a healer, his hands lying on my stomach. "You're not digesting soy," he said. "Not getting enough protein." He removed his hands and looked me in the eye. "Eat salmon."

But I stuck to my guns, believing a vegetarian diet was the best course of action. Another two weeks passed.

I was sitting in the office of a medical doctor, one of those rare breeds who incorporate alternative medicine in his practice. "New studies have shown that a vegetarian diet is not the best diet for humans," he said, reviewing my lab results. "I myself was a vegetarian for twenty years. I changed when I learned that my body was getting too many carbs and not enough protein."

I sat across from him, my arms folded across my chest. "I want to remain a vegetarian," I responded.

He knit his brow and leaned across the desk. "Well, it's up to you. If you stay with this diet, stay at this weight, down the line you'll likely get diabetes or heart disease or something worse."

Shaken, I left the doctor's office and climbed into my car. I didn't want to get diabetes or heart disease. *But if I change, what about Mark? He's been a vegetarian for over twenty years. What will he think?*

I picked up my cell phone, punched in his number, and babbled away, tears stinging my eyes.

"You know," he said thoughtfully, "I'm also feeling tired, like I'm not getting enough nutrition. I've actually been thinking about changing over for a year now."

And so we changed our diet and our energy levels increased although the universe practically had to hit me over the head for me to do it.

Life Is Not Random

The basic premise of synchronicity is that life is not at random; that the people we meet and the circumstances we find ourselves in, are there for a purpose.

Synchronicity, the hand of fate, had brought a wonderful man into my life. We married in the fall of 1994 and began a new life together. Our home portrayed our personalities: his pottery collection, my baskets. His Buddha figures, sand paintings of Native American shamans, and totem animals carved in wood or stone. My papyrus of Isis, figures of Kwan Yin, crystals and books and fuzzy stuffed animals.

I introduced healthy eating, natural medicines, and traveling abroad. He taught me about photography and the basics of golf, took me to watch the Giants play baseball in San Francisco, and shared the music of his favorite musicians: Tears for Fears, Yes, Genesis, and John Mellencamp.

I got him interested in Indian curries, Greek spanikopita, Thai noodles, Mexican fajitas, and aromatic Persian rice. He shared his love of pizza, lasagna, eggplant parmesan and anything chocolate.

We shared our love for nature, travel, watching movies, and reading each night in bed. We flowed easily together, as if we'd been lifelong friends. And I knew. Felt it in my bones that we were meant to be together, that this was the fulfillment of a sacred contract, that together, our souls would soar.

THE FLIP SIDE OF SYNCHRONICITY

Synchronicity does not always bring pleasurable events into our lives. Sometimes it shakes us up, creating challenges and difficulties for us to overcome so that we may tap into our hidden potentials and talents. By working through these challenges, we spiritually grow and evolve, raising our vibrations in the process. Although it may not seem so at the time we are in the thick of them, these challenges are, in reality, opportunities for growth.

In the spring of 1995, rumor had it that the program I was working for at the University of Hawai'i would be cancelled. I had to face the possibility that I might soon become unemployed, an experience I had never dealt with before. The manager at Mark's company had left and his son was reluctantly running the company and things were not going very well. If I lost my job, life could get tough.

At work, my colleagues hustled to get their resumes and letters of recommendation together and make contacts to find new positions. I meditated and sought inner guidance—ESL teaching jobs were rare on the island. Following my colleagues' lead seemed the logical thing to do, but inner spirit continuously urged me *not* to take such action. My intuitive guidance clearly said that I need not be concerned and that I would continue to work in the same location. I assumed this meant that the university would not cancel the program.

Hearing my inner voice was one thing. Accepting the information as truth, especially in this situation, was easier said than done. My logical mind was in direct conflict with the guidance of my spirit. A war raged within me. It was like the little angel and devil on the shoulders of cartoon characters. The little devil, my ego, would argue: "Have you lost your mind? Get real! You need to do what it takes to find a new job. Stop dallying."

The little angel, my spirit, would say: "You need do nothing. Everything will be fine. You will continue to work at this place. You have nothing to fear."

I felt pulled, wrenched this way and that, but finally decided to trust Spirit in spite of my fears. To distract my logical mind from the worries and concerns of my colleagues, I focused my attention and energies on writing a cookbook. I also registered in a distance learning program and began studying nutritional science, another passion of mine.

With the housing market slump, the real estate appraisal company where Mark worked was going downhill. Most of the other employees had moved on. Mark considered looking for another position, but his gut feeling told him to stay put. After watching a TV ad, he ordered a series of self-improvement tapes to help him focus and make changes in his life. Ecstatic that Mark was willing to do inner work, something he is normally disinclined to do, I decided to join in and go through the program with him. Each night, we'd turn off the TV, listen to the tape, and do the exercises. We followed the program religiously, working through our issues and beliefs about money, creating new goals, coming up with steps to achieve these goals, and focusing on change. I sensed a shift happening inside me, feeling more confident and optimistic as we completed the program. I began to trust the guidance of my inner spirit and believed that everything would turn out okay.

To my shock and disbelief, in late spring, 1995, the dean informed us that the ESL program would be cancelled at the end of the summer session. My mouth felt as dry as sand. I dragged myself home and soaked in the tub, my mid-section feeling like I'd swallowed a boulder. *Did I make it all up? Was the inner guidance just a delusion to make myself feel better?* I took a couple of deep breaths to calm myself. A comforting energy washed over my body, enveloping me like a warm, loving hug. The inner voice came loud and clear: *Everything will turn out just fine. You will continue to work at this place.*

But this doesn't make sense. I've just been handed my pink slip! Baffled, I asked Spirit for a sign. Within minutes, my husband opened the door and sat on the side of the tub. I blurted out the bad news, struggling to keep my composure. He held my hand, smiled warmly, and said, "Don't worry, sweetie. I have good news." He paused, a boyish twinkle in his green eyes. Sitting up straight on the side of the tub, he squared his shoulders, and announced: "You are looking at the new owner of SEVCO Appraisers!"

I thought my jaw would hit the side of the tub. "But how?"

"Remember when we went to Kona and talked to the owner and I offered to take over since his son wasn't really interested in running the company?"

"So they agreed?"

"Yep. They said I can buy it from them by paying a small percent monthly." Mark grinned widely. As owner of SEVCO Real Estate Appraisers, he knew that our financial situation would greatly improve since the company was well-established and Mark was hardworking and diligent. In other words, losing my job was, suddenly, not even a concern.

That was a good sign, God. Thanks!

"This calls for a celebration," I said, forgetting about my earlier dilemma.

And so, we celebrated our good fortune and dined on eggplant parmesan and red wine at Pescatore's Italian restaurant in Hilo, on the exact same day I'd been handed my pink slip from work.

It didn't stop there. A couple of weeks after the end of the semester, the ESL program started up again under the administration of the community college and I was called back to teach for the fall session. Oddly enough, since the university and the community college shared a campus, the classrooms were in the same location as before. To top it all off, six months later, due to another series of synchronistic events, I became the program director with a higher salary.

In this new position, the challenges were never-ending: teachers complained about each other; students complained about teachers; one teacher insisted I do things her way and would get indignant and irate when I didn't; Swiss and Japanese roommates burst into tears in my office, insisting they couldn't live together for one more day; I rushed one student to the emergency room after an urgent call from the school nurse worried that her allergies might constrict her breathing; and I held another's hand at the dentist while she had her tooth removed. I had to hire teachers each session, making the tough decisions of who would be in the best interest of the students and the program, and who would not get an assignment.

Why am I doing this? I asked my inner spirit, who had nudged me into this position. I was in my mid forties and believed I should be slowing down, not working harder than I'd ever done in my life.

You are learning to be a leader, came the reply.

Leader of whom? Of what?

You will know when the time comes.

The dean sent me to national conferences to learn how to do my job better. I traveled to Phoenix, New York, Vancouver, and Washington D.C. and learned about immigration regulations, marketing, program management, and new technologies in the field. Through much trial and error, I finally managed to put together a stellar teaching team.

I wanted to be sure that I was providing these international students with the best materials, teachers, and support services possible, so I decided to seek accreditation for the program. And even though I got stuck with the lion's share of the work, I managed to get national accreditation for the program, a stamp of approval from my professional peers that we were on the right track. This helped me realize that I was capable of much more than I had given myself credit for.

Meanwhile, Mark's appraisal business flourished and our financial situation improved dramatically. All unsecured debts were paid off; we both drove brand new cars, and we took yearly vacations out of state. We purchased land on the Big Island and designed our own home. Mark became his own contractor and did all the finish work, building beautiful oak kitchen cabinets with tiled counter tops, bathroom fixtures, tiled floors, bookshelves, and a hutch with glass doors, all in meticulous detail.

"How did you learn to do all this?" I asked.

"I read books and used common sense," he said. "Besides, I had a project like this in New England. Had a home built and did all the finish work on weekends. Sold it for a tidy profit."

In early 1996, about a year and a half after we married, we moved into our new home. Mark made sure it was beautiful and secure, as if I were a precious jewel that he wanted to encase and protect.

I smile to myself as I recall that inner struggle, when I wondered why my inner guidance was making no logical sense, telling me not to look for a new job when I was clearly being laid off. And yet, by listening to that still small voice in spite of the fears, miracles happened.

The mystery of synchronicity had always been working in my life. All I had to do was pay attention to the signs, listen to my inner guidance, and trust.

Chapter Eleven: Making the Choice

Reality is merely an illusion, albeit a very persistent one.

– Albert Einstein

Life was good. I had a wonderful marriage, a beautiful home, a good job. I lived in paradise; interesting people from all over the world showed up at my university office door; and even though I lived on a rock in the middle of the Pacific Ocean, whatever I required to spiritually grow and evolve would show up in the form of people, books, tapes, videos, spiritual teachers, groups, workshops, and seminars.

Mark's company thrived and we took regular vacations full of fun and adventure. Framed photos of these trips decorated the walls of our home: Haleakala on Maui, Lake Louise in Banff, Canada, The Grand Canyon in Arizona, Mt. McKinley and the Kenai River in Alaska, a harbor in the Bahamas, Disneyworld in Florida, Lake Tahoe in California, the Grand Tetons in Wyoming, Rockport in Massachusetts, the opera house in Sydney, Australia, a forest path in the mountains of New Zealand. Like a dream come true, I had everything I had ever wanted, needed, or desired. For the first time in my life, I was truly happy.

It was March, 2002. I woke up, as usual, to the song of zebra doves. A soft rain pattered on the metal roof as I stumbled into the bathroom to get ready for work. I glanced out the window into the back yard, vibrant with wild orchids and o'hia trees blooming with bright red lehua blossoms.

Looking into the oval-shaped bathroom mirror, I was nonchalantly brushing my teeth when water began to dribble out one side of my mouth. I grabbed a towel and wiped off the dribble, only to discover more watered-down toothpaste oozing out of my mouth and down my chin. I tried to stop the ooze, but couldn't. The right side of my face felt odd, numb, like I'd just come back from the dentist and the Novocain had yet to wear off.

What the hell? I stared in the mirror, smiled, frowned, stretched my mouth from side to side. The right side did not have as full a range of motion as the left side. I thought about Corinne, a colleague who was afflicted with Bell's Palsy, a temporary paralysis of the face due to an inflammation of the facial nerve. Anxiety stabbed my gut.

No! This can't be happening!

I saw my doctor that same day and informed him that I thought I had Bell's Palsy. He looked at me with a smirk. "If you're right, that is the mildest Bell's I've ever seen." He rose and examined my ear, positive that the paralysis was due to an ear infection. "Your ear is totally clear," he said, a baffled look on his face.

He sat on the chair across from me, his expression more concerned now. "Smile," he said.

I managed a crooked smile. The right side barely moved.

"Okay, now try to close your right eye."

I closed my right eye, but not all the way.

"Try and squint," he said, leaning forward.

I managed to squint, but barely.

"I guess you do have Bell's," he admitted with a shake of his head, and prescribed me six days of Prednisone, a steroid to inhibit the inflammation.

"Most people, about 80%, completely recover," he said. "You should be back to normal in five weeks or so."

Yet, while Corinne had woken up one morning and believed she had had a stroke, my Bell's came on gradually, in the course of about three to four days. At the end of this period, to my horror and disbelief, the entire side of my right face was completely paralyzed.

Nothing can prepare a person to deal with a situation like this—one's physical appearance, the face she shows to the world, so dramatically altered in such a short time. Humbled and helpless, I had no choice but to surrender to the experience and try to keep perspective—there was a lesson here, a reason for this, and I needed to pay attention.

As I battled with my emotions and negative thoughts, Mark searched for a way to help make me feel better. He booked a room for the weekend at the Waiakaloa Hilton, a magnificent resort on the western side of the Big Island with waterways, a lagoon, dolphins, waterfalls, and exquisite artwork from around the world. He suggested I use the spa and get any treatment my heart desired, so I allowed myself to be pampered in the world-class Kohala Spa with facials, massage, jacuzzi, steam room, sauna, and the works.

At sunset, we enjoyed a seven-course Chinese dinner, overlooking the waterway with boats taking passengers to and from their rooms, the sun setting over the Pacific Ocean painting the sky in pinks and reds. I sat across from Mark, half my face frozen and expressionless, conscious of one eye larger than the other, staring wide open, unable to blink. The right side of my mouth drooped. I felt like one of Dr. Frankenstein's bizarre creations.

My husband smiled at me from across the table. "You're my beautiful wife."

I choked, scrambled to keep my composure. Could it be true? Was Mark actually seeing past my outer appearance into the real me? I intellectually knew that we were all, in truth, spirit in body form, but it was not until I saw my spirit reflected in the eyes of my beloved that it truly hit home.

A couple of days later the pain began. Fiercely independent and proud of it, I found myself in a situation where I could not totally take care of myself due to the extreme pain in my ear and head. The doctor's prescriptive medication barely took the edge off the pain, so I had no choice but to surrender to my husband's care. I could only watch, helpless and vulnerable, while he made me food or brought me water and pain medicine. My heart melted seeing the pain in his eyes. He wanted to do something, *anything,* to make this better, to make it all go away.

I have never considered myself a vain person. Although I pay attention to my appearance, the time I spend on grooming is minimal in comparison with most women. I remember that, during my first year in Hawai'i, I got up one day to get ready for work and went to the bathroom to put on my makeup. Eye shadow brush in one hand, I suddenly froze, feeling that somehow this was not right. It just wasn't me. I stared at my face in the mirror. *Why am I putting an artificial face on myself?* I thought, rather amused that this had never occurred to me before. *There is nothing wrong with my face just the way it is.* I tossed the shadow brush in the trash. It felt good. I gleefully collected all my makeup: lipstick, mascara, powder, pencil and blush—and tossed them into the trash. I looked back in the mirror and smiled. *If anyone doesn't like me just the way I am, tough!* I turned on my heel and left for work, feeling like what I had just done was much more significant than throwing away the makeup. I had thrown away the mask I showed to the world. And while in later years, I did use make up for special occasions like weddings or a cruise formal night, it never again became a daily routine.

In the days following the make-up purge, nylons, high-heeled shoes, and any clothes that were not completely comfortable or made of natural fibers followed the makeup into the trash.

I'll wear only comfy clothes with patterns and colors I like, clothes that make me feel good inside. Who gives a hoot about the current fashion? It's all made up anyway.

From here on end, I will show the real me to the world.

But now, afflicted with facial paralysis, I found myself consistently staring in the mirror as if overnight I had been transformed into Narcissus, infatuated with the reflection of my own image, searching desperately for any small sign of movement or change. Coincidentally, I went to see the movie *Vanilla Sky* in which actor Tom Cruise played a man who had difficulty dealing with a facial deformity caused by an accident. I could relate.

Research on the Internet just made things worse when I realized that some people do not totally recover. I faced the fear of possibly looking like a freak for the rest of my life—a humbling experience that made me drop to my knees and pray for guidance.

"What if I don't heal?" I asked Mark, voicing my deepest inner fear.

"It's not an issue for me," he said, wrapping me in warm, loving arms. "I'm concerned about how *you* are feeling, how this is affecting you psychologically," he added, his eyes a mixture of love and concern.

I melted into his embrace, placing my head on his heart. *Could this be true? Could a man really love a woman beyond her appearance? Could this man love the real me, the being inside?*

I stood back and looked up into his Irish green eyes, his long, dark eyelashes, his trim peppered beard. I always thought he had kind eyes.

"You do whatever you need to take care of yourself, sweetie. Don't worry about me," he emphasized. And he meant it.

* * * * *

The following day, I was at the supermarket check-out counter.

"Would you like a box for this plant?" the salesclerk asked.

"A box would be fine." I was having difficulty pronouncing my b's and p's, so I sounded a little funny.

"Excuse me?"

"A box is okay," I said.

She repeated her question, dragging out each word with exaggerated pronunciation, then looked up at me with a grin.

Oh, my God! She thinks I'm a derelict.

"Forget the box," I said, my voice tinged with anger. Grabbing my plant and bags of groceries, I stormed out of the store.

This same scenario repeated itself everywhere I went: stores, restaurants, gas stations, even the office staff at work who should have realized that my *face* was paralyzed, not my brain! Infuriated by this condescending treatment disguised as "help," I developed a real compassion for individuals who were afflicted with permanent disabilities. I now understood what they had to deal with.

On the other hand, I was amazed and confounded by how much value I had placed on my intellect and, even more so, on people seeing me as intelligent. I had identified who I was with my intellect, my level of education, and my job. This realization unraveled me, pulling all the pieces apart so I could get a good look at who I really was inside, making me understand that I was more than my physical appearance, more than my intellect, and that the "me" inside was still there, in tact, just as it had always been, regardless of my outer appearance and people's perception of me.

This understanding was an epiphany that changed me in a profound way. I don't believe I will ever look at other people the same way again, regardless of race or color, whether they are thin or fat, young or old, or have any kind of physical deformity or disability. Although I always knew this intellectually, I now truly believe and understand that one's outer appearance has nothing to do with the person inside. With Bell's Palsy, it finally hit home.

Although there is no treatment (other than steroids to suppress the immune system and reduce the inflammation and nerve damage), and in most cases Bell's heals by itself, I embarked on a healing process involving acupuncture and emotional healing work. I added chiropractic manipulation, herbs, nutrition, and physical exercise to boost my immune system and increase my chances of healing. While all this healing work most likely improved my overall health, I am not sure if it did much to help the Bell's, but at least it made me feel like I was doing something, actively participating in my recovery.

In spite of all these efforts, the healing process was excruciatingly slow.

What We Focus on, Expands

I had learned years ago that I had to focus my thoughts on what I wanted in life, as the saying goes: "Energy flows where attention goes." I had practiced this concept for years and preached it to those around me. Nevertheless, when a challenge like Bell's Palsy hit, all my training and understanding of spiritual matters flew out the window. For over a year, I focused on the Bell's, the deformity, and problems with my weight. What do you think I got? More Bell's and more weight!

A war raged within me. On one level, I knew that everything in life happens for a reason, that this was only a learning process; that I needed to look for the teaching, the lesson. On the other hand, the physical reality of the deformity challenged me beyond anything I had ever experienced, even more so than my bout with cancer over two decades before.

And while this inner conflict was going on, I still went to work, took care of my home and my husband, and presented a strong face to the world. Everyone thought I was dealing with it well. Everyone except Mark. He knew me too well.

I worried constantly and stared at my own image so much that he threatened to throw out every mirror in the house. "Stop obsessing over this," he'd say emphatically. "You're just making things worse. Try to go on with your life and be happy!"

Deep down, I knew he was right, but I couldn't get myself to stop. It was like an addiction, a horrible obsession. I'd stare at my face, looking at every nuance; the most minute movement, even though I had done the same thing but an hour before.

As I look back, I realize that this inner war had already been well underway for quite some time prior to the Bell's Palsy. Part of me believed in the ethereal, intangible reality of Spirit, the guidance of my inner self, the idea that I was on this earth for a mission and a purpose. Another part of me declared the whole thing a figment of my overactive imagination and tried to convince me to get real. Both sides of me, call them spirit and ego, or intellect and intuition, were in mortal combat; neither making any progress, until, finally, there was a stalemate and half of my face froze. My body and spirit displayed this truth in a very literal way I would not miss. I could no longer sit on the fence. I had to either accept the reality of my spiritual beliefs and focus on my life's mission or let go of it all and live my life out interacting with the physical world only.

It was time to make the choice. This was my next wake-up call.

Fifteen months after the Bell's had begun, I had healed about 70%. While people told me I looked fine, each time I saw myself in the mirror, a deformed human being stared back at me, as if I had been transferred to the Bizzaro world in the *Superman* comic books. One eye was smaller than the other. One side of my face looked like I had been to the dentist a few hours before and the anesthesia had not totally worn off.

I had exhausted all avenues of healing that I could think of or had found through research on the Internet, in both traditional and alternative medicine. I had done emotional release work with rebirthing, hypnosis, and shamanic healing. Now, I was sitting in the office of a neurosurgeon.

"We used to think that after six months, the nerves would heal as much as they were going to and that was it. We have since discovered that the face and its nerves are a living system." He seemed reluctant to say more. I figured he meant that there were possibilities, but no guarantees.

"Is there anything you can do for me?" I asked, my face brightening.

His expression shifted. I realized that he had no further game plan—nothing else to offer.

"Some people do have surgery," he said, "but neurological surgery is a major operation and dangerous.

If, after surgery, a Bell's patient looked like you do now, the surgery would be considered a success." He pushed my hair back to get a better look at my face. "It doesn't look bad," he added.

My stomach clenched. *Is this the end of the line? Am I stuck looking like this for the rest of my life?*

The kind doctor gently pulled up one side of my face. "If it really bothers you, you could always try plastic surgery. Nothing drastic. Just a little lift here in order to balance things out."

I scrunched my face. *Plastic surgery? Doesn't that fall into the realm of shallow Hollywood characters who've done so much plastic surgery and Botox that they don't look human anymore?*

The neurologist gave me the names of two surgeons in Kailua-Kona, on the other side of the island. I thanked him and left his office, dismissing the whole idea as preposterous.

I slumped in my lazy-boy chair at home, tears rolling down my cheeks. *Why hasn't it totally healed? I have learned to accept unconditional love. I have learned that I am not my intellect; that I am not my physical appearance. I have learned that people are more than their physical appearance and I need to refrain from judgment. I have learned that I need to keep my mind, body, and spirit in balance and harmony. I have gotten off the fence and accepted the reality of Spirit. What else do I need to learn?*

No answer came. Maybe I was too emotional to hear it. Maybe I was not ready to deal with the final lesson at that time. Maybe part of the process was in not knowing.

I wasn't sure how to tell Mark about this, so I blurted it out in a fit of irritation. "Can you believe this guy? He suggested plastic surgery! Can you imagine *me* getting plastic surgery?"

Mark listened carefully. He was quiet, contemplative for a few moments. He turned and looked straight in my eyes: "Well, if this is something you want to do, sweetie, don't be concerned about the money. We're doing fine and it's not even an issue. I'm more concerned about your psychological well-being. If this will help you feel better, then let's do it."

I blinked with incredulity. I had been expecting agreement, a rebuttal of the doctor's preposterous suggestion. Shocked at his comments, I leaned back in my chair and flipped on the TV.

In the following days, the thoughts swirled through my mind. *Would I look like myself again? Maybe I'd look even younger! But surgery? This was not the "spiritual" thing to do. It would be harsh on my body. An invasion. How could this be right? Yet, what was the alternative? Maybe it was justified since it was "corrective" surgery due to an illness rather than one of pure vanity.* A week later, after a meditation, I asked for guidance.

If this will help your self-value, your sense of self-esteem, then do it. The voice was gentle, soothing.

What? But how can this be a "spiritual" thing to do?

There is no judgment. It is only a tool. If the tool will assist you in accepting yourself, use it.

But won't it harm my body?

Your body will heal. Your value of self, on the other hand, is most important to fulfilling your life's purpose.

My head spun. There was no judgment. The surgery was a tool, not unlike any other tool we may use to improve ourselves and fulfill our life's purpose. This information astounded me. I realized I had divided the universe into the "spiritual" and the "mundane." These were nothing more than thoughts of duality—the belief that there were some things in the universe that were separate from God. These divisions were only in my mind, not in reality, not in truth.

Suddenly, I understood many of the people who used this tool of surgery. It may not all be pure vanity or shallowness, although that was still a possibility. It could very likely be a tool to help them improve their self-acceptance. The acceptance of self could raise their vibration and propel them on their spiritual path. *Wow!*

The surgery would require at least four weeks healing time. Due to a synchronicity of events, I had changed my position at the university the year before and now had summers off—this being my first summer vacation in my 31-year career. I had the time. I had the money. I had the support of both my husband and my inner spirit. I made the choice.

On June 4th, 2003, I succumbed to surgery. Mark was by my side when I woke. I sensed the warmth of his hand on my arm; saw the concern in his face. I was still too drowsy to care about anything.

We rented a condo near the doctor's office. In spite of the fact that his appraisal company was going through a very busy period, Mark dropped it all to stay by my side. He sat on the bed next to me, gently cleaning my sutures with Q-tips and covering them with antibiotics.

"How about some soup?" he asked.

"Soup and butterscotch pudding."

"Got it." He hitched his pants and sauntered off towards the kitchen. I flipped through channels with the remote.

I had planned to avoid mirrors for the first week, but the condo had a bathroom mirror that spanned the entire wall. I stared at myself with horror and disbelief. I looked like a puffer fish who had taken a beating. Dark bruises surrounded my eyes and neck. Blue eyes no more than slits. I felt like hell. *What have I done!*

Mark returned from a grocery trip and presented me with a small gift: a pretty fairy with long hair and sparkling wings. "This is what you look like to me," he said, planting a gentle kiss on my cheek. "You're my beautiful wife."

I look like I've been run over by a truck and he thinks I'm beautiful? Maybe it is really possible for humans to love the soul of a person, I thought as we lay on the bed together and watched a movie.

I thought of all the different opportunities that had presented themselves in my life, opportunities to open my heart and experience love and compassion, like when I made friends with Chris's partner, Peter, or the time I held the young man dying of AIDS in my arms. Other opportunities had included distributing flowers in a nursing home, throwing a baby shower for a colleague, and giving small gifts of appreciation to people at work. These experiences of giving and sharing helped me spiritually grow and blossom, but it wasn't until I met Mark that I actually experienced being on the *receiving* end of love and compassion. It was Mark who opened the deeper levels of my heart. It was Mark who taught me how to love.

Mark sat next to me in bed, propped up by a mound of pillows, sipping wine, as he watched the movie on TV. I reached over and gently placed my hand on his.

* * * * *

Several months later, I was mostly healed. Now, I saw a more balanced face in the mirror. This new image lifted my spirits and provided the impetus necessary for me to make the choice to follow the path of Spirit, however it may unfold.

"I'll do it!" I cried out loud, to God, to the Universe, to the Divine Consciousness, the heavenly hosts, to anyone who wished to listen. Face raised to the heavens, hands held high, with as much conviction as I could muster up, I declared: "I, Patricia Anne Panahi, here and now, declare my intent to fulfill my higher purpose on earth. This is my solemn vow."

I paused, feeling a surge of energy. "And I request assistance in completing my mission, in whatever form appropriate."

A loving feeling washed over me as I left the house and went about my day.

Seek the Answers Within

When we begin grade school, we are given a basic reader. Once we master that reader, we graduate to the next level and receive more appropriate materials. What if the sacred teachings we received centuries ago were the primers, materials appropriate for that day and age and that particular stage of human development? What if we were ready for the next level, but we remain stuck because we are attached to our "primer" materials and enamored with the personality of the original messengers?

What if the next set of materials doesn't come from an enlightened individual or prophet, but instead we're all required to find the answers within ourselves? What if connecting and listening to the Spirit within is the next stage of our evolutionary process?

To use Joseph Campbell's metaphors, it is no longer appropriate to wait for a hero to come and save us; we are each responsible to walk the hero's path—the path of transformation.

Using Discernment

Maybe, just as we are each created unique, down to the iris of our eyes and our DNA, we each have to walk our spiritual paths and find God in our own special way. Maybe one's spiritual path and purpose in life is unique to that individual; and whether a person chooses to follow the teachings of a particular spiritual master/prophet, or his/her own sense of spirituality, the path, the process must remain open, fluid, and ever changing. Maybe the main point is for our minds and hearts to expand so we progress and see truth from different vantage points and levels of understanding. All the holy scriptures of the world, all the teachings of the great masters, all the traditions and their varied practices, all are there as guideposts, signs that lead us in the direction of truth that resides deep within our souls, within the human heart.

If the above premise is true and our spiritual development now rests within ourselves, where would this leave the thousands of religious leaders in the world--the priests, the gurus, the imams, the monks? What would happen to the many religious organizations around the globe? Attending a seminary, studying religious texts, or practicing a set of prescribed rituals does not necessarily lead to enlightenment, although these actions may be steps in one's individual path of transformation.

In centuries past, few people had the ability to read and write. Only those with this ability such as priests, monks, mullahs, and holy men, could study the sacred texts, gain knowledge unknown to the average person, and interpret the messages for the masses. The 21st century is a new world. Most people can read sacred texts for themselves. Sacred texts from numerous religions and traditions are readily available in most countries. And since many of these texts were not written by the original spiritual master, but by their students, examination and reinterpretation of these sacred texts with an open mind can provide opportunities for followers to expand their consciousness beyond dogma and doctrine and into the truth and essence of what these masters were truly teaching. Even now, there are teachers on earth who have attained a high degree of enlightenment and understanding of spiritual matters. These teachers can guide and inspire us to reach our inner selves, but, I believe, once we make a clear connection to our own spirits, it is that still small voice we should follow above all others.

The new curriculum was clear to me now:
Use discernment and listen to the small voice within.

Chapter Twelve: Your Mission, Should You Choose to Accept It, Is...

It is good to have an end to journey toward, but it's the journey that matters in the end.

— Ursula K. LeGuin

After healing from the surgery, I found myself with renewed energy to make changes in my life. The mild spasm in one side of my face was a constant reminder to be diligent and focus on balance. I increased my level of exercise, improved my diet, began to meditate regularly, paid attention to the promptings of my inner spirit about what I needed to do next in my life's work, focused myself with affirmations and visualizations, and began the first draft of this book.

Something was awakening inside of me, a passion, a fire, an inner spiritual force that propelled me forward.

The Hindus call this energy *Prana,* the Japanese know it as *Ki,* and the Chinese refer to it as *Qi (chi).* The Navajo call this energy that connects all things *sa'a naghari bike'e hozho* while the Hawaiians refer to it as *Mana*. It is the life force energy within each human being and all of creation, a force we can connect with and consciously increase. I had tapped into this energy and it was beginning to grow.

<u>Do I Make a Difference?</u>

Fully committed to my spiritual path, my inner fire blazing, I was prepared to take on new challenges, dive headfirst into whatever Spirit laid before me. But, at the same time, my deepest doubts and fears crept to the surface, like dark tendrils, grabbing and clutching at every opportunity. *Do you really think you make a difference?* My ego whispered. *Do you really think you matter? What have you done to affect anyone's life?*

A shiver ran up my spine. *Could it be true? Was my existence still as meaningless as when I had gotten cancer? Have I done anything of significance?* I remembered reading in one of the Kryon books by Lee Carroll that it is important for us to focus on our own spiritual growth and development. By balancing our own bodies and energy fields, we affect everyone around us. They, in turn, affect others. In other words, it is not "selfish" to focus on our own spiritual growth and understanding, as some would have us believe. By raising our own vibration, we raise the vibration of the whole.

So, if nothing else, by releasing my own fears and raising my vibration, I am affecting everyone I come into contact with. I am making a difference, even though it may not be apparent to others.

Are you, now? Said the voice of my ego, that little devil sitting on my shoulder.

Ego haunted me, teased me, goaded me, ridiculed my attempts at writing the first draft of this book, bringing up every doubt, every fear, every insecurity in the process. Fear that I wasn't good enough, that I couldn't write worth squat, that no literary agent worth her salt would want to represent me, that no publisher would want to publish me, that I was wasting my time, that I was delusional.

What do you know about spirituality? Ego whispered in my ear. *Who would want to read your material, anyway? You have nothing to say.*

One afternoon, after a long meditation, I clearly heard the voice of my inner spirit:

It is part of your contract, your purpose, to express what you have learned. You have much to share. Much to teach. The writing of this book is a medium you have chosen to bring forth what is burgeoning from within, seeking expression.

Me? But I don't know what to say. I haven't even made a difference in anyone's life all these years.

I had barely finished my question when the images came, flooding my mind in Technicolor detail:

A woman is sitting in the back room at The Light Spot. She is sipping herbal tea and reading a metaphysical book. Her energy shifts, her aura changes from blues to white and gold.

The scene shifts. I am embracing a man during a rebirthing session as tears wash away his pain. Love energy flows from my heart to his. He becomes calm, peaceful

Shift again. I am at my previous job, ready to leave. I sit across from my supervisor, a dynamic woman stuck in a job too small to contain her. She places her hands flat on the table, leans forward, and looks me straight in the eye. "I was feeling stuck here, yet everyone kept advising me to stay with the system, to consider the retirement benefits. But you think differently than other people. You inspired me and caused me to see that I'd made this place my box. Thank you, Patti."

I ran into her three years later. She had moved to the west coast and was back in Hawai'i for a visit. "How's your job there?" I asked. "I love it!" she said with a big smile.

Okay, so I've affected a few people, I admit, still not totally convinced.

The following day, a colleague stopped to chat in the office. "You don't know how much you've affected Corinne," she said. "It's the little things you do, like taking her out to experience a new food, bringing her fruit or small gifts from your trips. These things are more important to her than you realize. She's learning, changing, beginning to take better care of herself instead of always taking care of everyone else."

Hmmm.

And then, out of the blue, I receive this e-mail at work:

> *Dear Patty,*
>
> *I hope this is the Patty Panahi who used to own a coffeehouse/bookstore in Hillcrest in the mid 1980's. If so, Hi! Remember me? The homeless guy who used to read Tarot cards and drive you bananas?*

Paul! Yes, I remember him. He used to sit at one of the tables with a sign that read: "Tarot Readings - $10." An open, friendly, wild sort of guy. Recalling a song I used to play at the shop, he had begun thinking about me and had decided to look me up.

> *Anyway, how are you doing? It appears you've done well for yourself.*
>
> *I'm doing very well. I finally got my act together and got off the streets. I went to tech school, got a diploma, and (eventually) a good job. I'm still clean and sober, too. I now own a condo in Scripps Ranch and have a great career. I'm respected in my line of work and I volunteer many hours in the community, including fundraising efforts.*
>
> *I remember those times at the store fondly. You provided me with a place to call "home" while I had none. You put up with me and showed me love when I had none left for myself. You actually cared. I want to thank you for being there and for showing me that hope is never lost.*
>
> *Thank you.*
> *Yours always,*
> *Paul A.*

Sitting in my office at work, I broke down and cried.

* * * * *

After twelve years and no word, I got a call from Peter who was visiting the island. Chris, Peter, and I got together for dinner and reminisced about old times.

"Do you remember when we started a twelve-step program at the Inner Visions Center?" Peter peered at me from across the table with those big blue eyes of his.

"Debtors Anonymous. Back in 1989. I remember." While I had never gotten myself into any serious debt, Peter thought it would be helpful to people, so I set the program up at the center and attended several meetings.

"Well," Peter said, grinning, "get this. That group is still meeting. They've moved to the building next door, but it's still going on, after all these years."

"Still going on? Huh."

"Yep. You never know what will happen when you set things in motion. It takes on a life of its own."

Peter's comments reminded me of my inner musings at the Light Spot after my encounter with the homeless man many years before:

If life has meaning and purpose, then it stands to reason that each and every one of us has a unique gift to give to the world—a contribution that will serve a higher cause.

Some people probably spend a lifetime in preparing for the gift they will give. Others may offer their gifts in small increments. Nevertheless, we all add to the richness of the human family; we all affect the world, regardless of appearances.

And so, in spite of ego, in spite of my doubts, my fears, my insecurities, and in spite of my busy schedule, I followed my inner promptings and plowed forward, stealing precious hours on weekends to begin the early draft of this book.

SEDONA CALLING

Calming my inner fears, I settled into life working as a program director at the university, writing this book, caring for my home, and enjoying time with my husband

and friends. I had planted roots in Hawai'i and it was finally beginning to feel like home.

We were planning our next vacation and Mark suggested we take a trip to the Southwest. He had visited the national parks in that area on a drive from New England to the west coast years before, and wanted to share these beautiful areas with me. Both surprised and intrigued that my husband, who had grown up and loved the lush green forests of New England, would be interested in the desert, I agreed to the trip.

Passing towering saguaros on our way from Phoenix to northern Arizona, I remembered a previous trip to the Southwest with my friend Chris and his rebirthing class back in the '80s. Chris had discovered a town called Sedona situated in an area sacred to the Native Americans and purported to have special energy spots or vortexes, spirals of electromagnetic energy that would enhance spiritual experiences. Upon arrival in Sedona, we were all dazzled by the towering red rock formations of buttes and pinnacles and deep canyons, stands of juniper pine and the refreshing waters of Oak Creek. A clerk at a New Age bookstore gave us directions to the vortexes, claiming that many people had visions while meditating there.

I recalled scrambling up the hill to Airport Vortex, a high mesa overlooking Sedona with panoramic red rock vistas. The palms of my hands felt tingly, like an electric current was running through them. At the vortex, the juniper pines, apparently in reaction to the spiraling electromagnetic energy, had grown twisted trunks and branches.

After a group rebirthing session on the Airport Vortex plateau, a woman in our party, Sharon, looked like a cartoon character who had just received an electric shock with about fifty strands of her hair standing straight up in the air.

Sharon, the practical, no-nonsense type, was having a hard time believing us as we each stepped forward to touch her flying hair in wonder. We now had physical proof that this place had a special energy unlike any other.

After remembering that Sedona experience, I turned to Mark and suggested we stop there for a few nights before venturing to the Grand Canyon. Mark, who had never experienced Sedona and was focused on getting to the Grand Canyon, reluctantly agreed.

Once again, the sheer beauty of the place captivated me. But this time, there was something more. I felt light, joyful, connected in this place. It felt *good* to be there. The heady scent of sage, the tingling sensation of the vortexes, the song of the cicadas at dusk, jack rabbits scuttling through the brush, the call of the coyote, and the beauty of the red rocks and Oak Creek canyon had wrapped around my soul. In addition to being sacred to the Native Americans of the area, Sedona was also a Mecca for spiritual seekers and students of metaphysics, with specialized stores on every corner offering books, crystals, psychic readings, aura photography, healings, and an array of spiritual paraphernalia. Numerous centers for personal growth and transformation offered classes and workshops in topics from Native American healing and Buddhist meditation to channeling angelic beings. I felt like I'd arrived at metaphysical Disneyland, with a populace that spoke of vortexes and spirit guides and personal transformation as a matter of course. While there were also many such people on the east side of the

Big Island, where I lived, they were not as visible as in Sedona—in Hilo, most kept to themselves. I realized how much I'd missed the daily stimulation, discussions, and experiences I used to have at the Light Spot. I missed being part of a progressive, open-minded spiritual community.

I sat cross-legged on a cliff at Airport Vortex, overlooking the town—red rock with juniper pine and cottonwood along the creek. Something stirred within, a feeling, a sensation, a memory. My vision softened, blurred. A phantom image overlaid my own, a Native American woman from long ago, a medicine woman. In that life, I loved to come to this overlook, to be alone, to meditate, to commune with nature. I held a special affinity for this place. It had been my sanctuary, my *spot*.

You will live here again, she whispered in my ear.

On the third day, I was packing to leave with a long face. We had a reservation at a Grand Canyon lodge and could stay in Sedona no longer. I left with a heavy heart, a part of me still clinging to the red rock cliffs.

* * * * *

Upon returning to the Big Island, I couldn't shake my attraction to Sedona and its people. Like a siren's call, Sedona had a magical grip on my soul. It was at this time that my inner guidance came loud and clear: *Your destiny is to live in Sedona.*

Not again! I cried. Visiting Sedona was one thing, but picking up and relocating there was a different ball of wax. Hadn't I done this once already when I moved from San Diego to Hawai'i? True, Sedona was a beautiful place, but I had a *life* in Hawai'i—I had roots: friends, a husband, a university career. Mark had golf buddies and a successful business. We didn't want to begin over again, especially at this age—I was now in my fifties—in a small town with few opportunities. In Hawai'i, we had a beautiful home on an acre of lush, green forest we both loved. We were financially comfortable as long as we kept working. Life was good. Why would I need to uproot myself and move again?

It is your destiny, chimed my inner spirit. *Your spiritual family is waiting to meet you there.*

Images flashed in my mind, images of me, on a stage, speaking to large groups of people about the books I'd written, about experiences I'd had. These images terrified me to no end.

Sedona was calling me. It called me through the voice of my spirit. It called me through visions. It called to me in my dreams. It wrapped itself around my heart and pulled at me like a puppet on a string.

I remembered when I first visited Hawai'i, when I was walking the path up at Akaka Falls and heard the voice of Spirit guiding me to move to the islands. *You will live here, but not for the rest of your life,* the voice had said. I had become comfortable in Hawai'i and forgotten about the second part of that message.

After much inner struggle, I finally let go of the fight and resigned to the fact that, at some point in the future, I would be moving to Sedona. How and when was still unclear. Fortunately, Mark liked Sedona, too, but would not be willing to move until he was ready to retire, which was years in the future; however, I didn't believe a decade in the future is what Spirit had in mind for me. And so I waited, quite impatiently, for events to shift, for new possibilities to emerge, for doors to open.

The Cave of Transformation

They say that when God closes one door, she opens another one. They never tell you that there can be a long hallway in between. Those are the times when you know something new is coming, glimpses of it teasing you through the open door. You also sense the old door closing as you sometimes gleefully, other times reluctantly, step towards the new one. And you walk, skip, trudge, wobble or crawl, yet that darn door is still out of reach like a frustrating dream, where you feel like you're trudging through a tar pit and no matter how hard you try, you never seem to get to your destination.

The hallway is one of the hardest places you can be.

Yet, maybe it's not just some long, dark hallway where we grope around blindly. *Maybe* it's a cave of transformation, a magical journey we willingly undertake lured by the Holy Grail on the other side of the door. *Maybe* entering this magical cave is only the first step, like a personal quest where we undergo a transformation of consciousness through a sequence of actions or series of trials like Joseph Campbell's "hero's journey." *Maybe* it requires a change in vibration, a shift in consciousness, before we are allowed to step through the other door.

I thought about times in my life when I had been in that "in between place." Times when I knew that some thing, some one, or some change was coming, so close I could taste it, smell it, sense its presence, yet at the same time it was as far away as another galaxy. I tried to think of the sequence of events, the trials, the shifts in consciousness that took place before I stepped through each door. I had had to *let go* of my pictures about moving to Hawai'i with Chris and Peter, let go of the way I thought things were supposed to turn out, take a leap of faith, and follow my own path. I had had to *transform* limited belief systems about myself and become more comfortable with who I was, become my *own woman,* for my soulmate to show up. I had had to *transmute* ideas and beliefs around money, abundance, and deservingness for my financial situation to change. Each time, outer change had followed an inner shift, a substantial transformation of consciousness.

I realized that finding love, a new job, money, a house or even physical healing were not really the goals as far as my spiritual development was concerned, but they *did* work well as lures to draw me into the cave of transformation and get me to do what needed to be done to raise my vibration. In other words, what happened during *the course of the journey* was the significant factor as far as my spiritual growth was concerned. Reaching my goal was just icing on the cake.

Now, I found myself in that darn hallway again. The need to express what was bulging and burgeoning within me, my experiences, my understandings and insights, could wait no longer. I craved the time and freedom to improve my writing craft, get my book written and published, then speak to others and share my spiritual process.

And Sedona still tugged at my heart. I'd heard of artists and spiritual seekers who just upped and quit their jobs and flew free, trusting in the Universe's care. Yet, while I was feeling the pull to Sedona, I was not getting a clear message to move there right away. I was also not willing for this move to be a financial struggle, not at this time in my life.

Flustered and confused, I didn't know how I was going to accomplish any of this. I had a good job at the University of Hawai'i, but it took much of my time and energy, leaving little to accomplish what my spirit was directing me to do. Nevertheless, I tried, writing like a mad woman on weekends, in spite of believing that my writing was crap and I had nothing to say. And since Sedona was a rather expensive place to live and Mark was not willing to begin a new career or business, I believed that I had to transform my beliefs about money and deservingness, taking it to a new level in order to make a move to Sedona a reality.

And so, I saved and invested and worked through my money beliefs using numerous modalities I had learned over the years. I prayed, focused, affirmed, visualized, and meditated. Months passed. Nothing changed. My book was making little progress. No additional finances presented themselves. I was stuck, feeling like a failure. Feeling like I did not have it within me to follow the directive of my soul. I needed help.

A few days later, while searching the Internet, I discovered Sedona Soul Adventures. Elation washed over me as I read through their website. I experienced that familiar tingling feeling of *rightness,* that wash of warmth. *Maybe these people can help me move forward.* Invigorated, I discussed the idea of going on a soul adventure with Mark later that day.

"They find the best people, healers and psychics and the like, and set you up with them," I exclaimed, bubbling with excitement. "I'm feeling stuck and this seems like just what the doctor ordered." I looked up into his bright green eyes, his long, curling lashes. His new goatee became him.

"I can go on a spiritual retreat during Spring Break," I continued. "I called and talked to Debra, my *angel guide*—that's a term they use at Sedona Soul Adventures—and she made suggestions for activities and healers I can choose from. She'll plan the whole thing out for me, make the appointments and tell me where to go. I just have to book my plane and hotel and show up."

"Sounds good," Mark said, raising one eyebrow. He flashed a disarming smile. "Go for it!"

SEDONA SOUL ADVENTURES

I sat on a cliff at Airport Vortex with Debra, my angel guide, overlooking the magnificent vista. *Interesting that I keep ending up at this spot.*

"Before we begin the meditation, I'd like you to declare your intention for this week," she said, her short, dark hair tossed about by the wind. It had been a calm, sunny day just minutes before, but the wind had picked up, seemingly out of nowhere.

I sat up straight, squaring my shoulders. "I want to clear all blockages so that I can express fully who I am and fulfill my purpose for being here," I declared with conviction.

Debra guided me into a meditation as the wind swirled around us, raw, primal. It billowed under my shirt and whipped my hair about, the energy dynamic, invigorating.

The meditation complete, we rose to leave. A forceful gust of wind raised a cloud of red dust, then softened. By the time we trekked the short distance to the car, it had completely died down. *Was this an omen, a foretelling of a powerful Sedona adventure to come?*

INTUITIVE READING

Claudia, a lively woman with short, bouncy hair and a German accent, hugged me warmly and welcomed me to her home. She guided me into a meditation, what she called my "inner house," and suggested I climb the stairs to the attic.

"You are going to meet your spirit guides," she said. "They may appear to you in any form."

The images were blurry at first, but became more visible with focus. "There are four," I said, excitement rising in my voice. I had heard my guides whisper in my mind. I had sensed their presence, a familiar warmth. But I had never *seen* them before.

"Greet the first one. Ask for a name."

"This guide is mostly white light, like an angel or a light being. He has a gentle face. His name is Mi-ka-el."

"Is he the archangel Michael?"

"No. He is connected to the archangel, but not him."

"What is the purpose of Mi-ka-el?"

"He guides and protects me."

"Okay, ask Mi-ka-el if he will give you a gift," she suggested.

I paused, watching Mi-ka-el in my minds eye. "Yes. A feather. He gave me a feather. He says when I receive the feather in physical form, it will be a sign of great wisdom and learning."

"Ask if he has any words for you at this time."

"He says *trust the process.*"

"That's good. Now go to the second one. What does it look like?"

I smiled. "This guide is an owl."

"An owl?"

"Yes." *An owl can see in the dark—see what is not visible to others, see the unseen. Hmm...*

"Okay," Claudia said. "Ask the owl why it is with you now."

I listened carefully, waiting for a response. "It says: 'I am here to help you connect more with nature.'"

"Does the owl have a gift for you?"

"Yes. Its gift, excuse me, *her* gift is also a feather."

"Ask if owl has anything to tell you at this time."

"Spend time in nature."

"Very good," she said. "Now go to the next guide."

"This is a Native American, but it's not clear. It's sometimes a man, then a woman, then a man again."

"This could be a person you knew in another life, once as a man, another time as a woman. Ask if this is so."

"Yes, that's right."

"Ask this guide to come to you in one form so you can see it clearly."

"Okay. It's a woman. An older Indian woman. This is the first time I'm meeting her."

A new spirit guide! I had asked the universe for help. Were these beings here in response to my request?

"Good. Ask why she is with you."

"Her job is to help with the synchronicity of events so that I can move to Sedona."

"Ask for her name."

I paused, all ears. "It's not clear."

"Okay. Greet the last guide."

"This is my Higher Self. She is giving me a warm hug." I opened my eyes and smiled warmly at Claudia, appreciating her help in actually *seeing* my guides rather than just sensing their presence.

"I feel that you need to meet a man named Jim Hawk," Claudia said. "He is a white man, not an Indian, but he knows many things. He's a shaman. He also does beautiful artwork." She showed me a wand with an intricately carved hummingbird on one end. "He also makes feather fans," Claudia added. "Ask your Higher Self if you are supposed to meet Jim Hawk."

I closed my eyes and asked the question. The answer came, loud and clear. *Yes!*

Claudia wrote down his telephone number on note paper shaped like a cat.

"We have a little time left. Do you have any questions?"

I shifted in my seat. "Yes, I do. I understand that I am supposed to write. I also know that I'm supposed to move to Sedona. What else can you tell me about my purpose, especially when I'm living in Sedona?"

Claudia closed her eyes for a moment, then opened them and looked straight at me. "All you are doing, by writing the book, by your time here, and similar activities, all that you are freeing within yourself, will help other people open their eyes to the light. You will sum up what you've learned and bring it to the ears of others, share your experiences. You will draw to you people who are stuck by other people's negativity. You will help them to get unstuck, to free them from the projections of others, parents, authority figures, society. Free them from attracting people who always stomp on them. You'll teach them self-empowerment."

I nodded, wondering how in the world I was going to manage that

"Your path right now is about your coming into wholeness, about self-empowerment, openness, oneness. Things are moving as they are supposed to be. Don't get impatient."

The session complete, I rose to leave. We hugged warmly. "Let me know when you are going to meet Jim Hawk," she said. "I'd like to come too."

SHAMANIC ASTROLOGY

"In this system," Sao said, gesturing with his hands, "each sign is an archetype, one of the twelve different ways a soul chooses to express itself in the world. We refer to them as tribes."

"Okay."

"The position of your moon tells us the tribe you came from in your past life. This is what you already know, what you have graduated in, what you're comfortable with. You have come from the Virgo tribe. This means that you were, in a sense, a priestess dedicated to the sacred work in whatever culture you might have been in. This sacred work is different from the priests of this culture who are not deep into the reality of the divine. This deep sacred work would have involved discovering the sacred patterns and developing ceremonies to keep humanity in the rhythm of those patterns, to keep us in the flow."

This astrology was very different from what I had experienced before. I sat up straight, all ears.

"Now within the Virgo tribe, you had the Capricorn job. Capricorn jobs are the responsible administrators, those who know the rules of the game. This position is that of the elder, of responsibility. It means that the energy you brought into this life is wisdom. Do you understand what I'm saying?"

I nodded. *A teacher, a business owner, a program director – positions of responsibility. Makes sense.*

"The past life lineage, which we probably do more than one lifetime, is what we're experts in. We're good at it. Comfortable with it. We have a tendency to continue with that past life experience instead of going forward in this life, but this doesn't get us anywhere, doesn't give us fulfillment in life. It's important to move forward and discover what your soul intended to do in this lifetime. Aligning yourself with that purpose, now that's powerful."

I sat on the edge of my seat. Here was the answer I was looking for.

Sao crossed his legs and continued. "Your rising sign shows your tribe in this life. You are a member of the Sagittarius tribe, the truth seekers, the ones who pass down the wisdom of the tribe. They are on an endless quest for truth. They need to be free like a bird to move around and look for truth wherever and whenever."

This is what I've been doing all my life-- seeking the truth. Could it be that the pattern of the stars and planets at the exact moment of birth actually create a blueprint of the soul's purpose?

"If they don't have that freedom of movement, they feel miserable, like they're in prison."

I was miserable in Iran—my freedom of movement severely limited. Nevertheless, I somehow found ways to discover and explore different ideas, beliefs, religions-- driven to seek the truth no matter the obstacles. Interesting!

"The vision quest was *made* for the Sagittarius tribe. Their job is to be always pushing the boundaries of truth, expanding the self. Never to feel complacent. Never feel like they have all the answers. Like Don Juan said to Carlos Castaneda: 'Clarity is an obstacle to spiritual truth.' We can get complacent until confusion shows up."

Could this be why I've never felt comfortable with any religion? They all seemed too confining, limited…

"Now your job in the Sagittarius tribe is a Cancer job. Cancer is the feminine energy as it manifests in the vibration of the mother, the nurturing aspect. This is a hands-on kind of work, very clannish, takes care of the ones that are hers. The Cancer job is also about keying in on family, being part of the revisioning and revising of the way we do family on earth."

"Now your strategy is the way you live your life, the tools you use to get where you need to go to fulfill your life plan. Living out the Pisces archetype is your main strategy, the way you propel yourself along."

I stared at him, confused.

"The key word for Pisces is world server. Serve the world in an unconditionally loving way. Compassion is another key word for Pisces—compassion for everybody. A great example of this is Mother Teresa. People all over the world would line up just to get a two-second hug from her. Are you getting what I'm saying here?"

"Not really." This stretched me. I didn't feel like Mother Teresa material.

Sao leaned forward. "Remember—you are enrolled in this mystery school in this lifetime. You're working at it. Investigating it. You haven't mastered it yet."

Sigh of relief. "I've been working on a book about my spiritual awakening. How does this fit into my life's purpose?"

Sao carefully reviewed my chart. "Mercury in your chart is in Aquarius—the archetype of awakening. This is how you think. You keep an eye on the bigger picture, have an overview of how things work. It's easy for you to grasp how our tiny lives on earth connect to the bigger picture. Writing this book is perfect for you. It's powerful. It helps expand the New Age sense of things. This is very much a part of your strategy—communicating. Helping other people who are trying to find their way by sharing yours."

"So my job is to share my experiences and make it real."

"Very important. Perfect for you. Pisces is about compassion and service to others. It can manifest in many ways. A book can reach people all over the world. Pisces is also about mysticism, visions, seeing beyond the veil."

"Can you give me any further details about my life's purpose?"

"Your tribe, Sagittarius, is about seeking truth, pushing the limits; your job is Cancer, the compassionate mother, your strategy is Pisces, the world server, the mystic. Now, it's up to you, however you do it. It could be that you help bring the truth about the Cosmic Mother out into the light, where she is no longer concealed from us. It could be that through you would be revealed aspects of the mother and ways of connecting to her that are brand new—very possible. Each person may be able to get his or her own unique connection with this information from you—maybe you'll write a book about it. With Mercury in Aquarius and all this Pisces energy, spirit could download a book to you in a day. The work won't be laborious; it'll be sweet, wonderful, easy."

I let out a giggle of relief. "Easy is good."

I don't have to be a Mother Teresa or a Gandhi or anyone else for that matter, I mused, smiling to myself. *I have my own path, my own mission, and I'll accomplish it in my own unique way.*

Emotional Clearing and Upliftment

I panted as I trudged up the steep driveway to my first appointment of the day. I wasn't sure what this session entailed—something about removing blockages—just what I needed. The first two Sedona Soul Adventure sessions had been great. I figured this one would be too.

Annie was practicing yoga postures on the deck. She looked about my age, give or take a few years, with a lithe and limber body, very different from my portly, sluggish self. *I'll get there,* I thought with conviction as I dragged myself up the stairs. Rob, a burly a man with a disarming smile appeared at the door to greet me.

As I stepped into their living room, a soft energy washed over me. I felt lighter, more peaceful and at ease. Large windows spread over two walls, filling the room with light and offering a view of the neighborhood and red rocks in the distance. I knew instinctively that this was a home of love and peace. This was also a place of spiritually awakened people. It felt *wonderful* just to be there.

In their downstairs healing room, I raised both arms, shoulder height, as Annie smudged me with sage. I said a silent prayer, requesting the presence and assistance of all my spirit guides, my Higher Self, and any angels or ascended masters who would like to assist me with this process. Immediately, the room filled with beings of light, ethereal, ghostly figures, their energies angelic. I smiled to myself, climbed onto the massage table, and closed my eyes. An object was placed on my chest. It felt heavy, like a flat stone, its warmth penetrating deep inside me. I figured it must be a crystal. *Odd. I've never heard of anyone heating a crystal before.*

I sensed movement and a soft breeze, as if I were being fanned by feathers. A gentle current flowed through my body in circular motion. Bahman's image appeared before me. Bahman, my first husband. I'd left him back in 1989.

Forgive him, came a soft voice in my head. I intuitively knew the forgiveness was not necessarily for anything that he had done, but for myself. In truth, all forgiveness is self to self. I was still holding on to the disappointment that he had not come through for me, that he had not lived up to my expectations of a husband, that I had not been able to depend on him, to count on him to be there for me.

Suddenly, it all became clear, like someone just flipped a switch in a dark room. The *strong* Patti needed to emerge; it was part of my path, my transformation. Bahman's soul contract with me was to help bring that part of me to the surface. If he had played the strong husband, taking care of my every need, I would never have gained the tools I needed to fulfill my life's purpose. In the early 1990s, he had returned to Iran and remarried. I recalled a recent picture I'd received by e-mail from a family member—a photo of his little girl. She was about ten years old with long, dark hair and a pretty smile. She had her father's eyes. What was her mission? Her purpose? What lives would she touch in her time on earth? What effect would her life have on her culture, her society, the world? If

Bahman and I had stayed together, she would have never been born. Yes! The pattern, the perfection, the divine plan of it all became crystal clear.

I acknowledged and thanked Bahman for the role he had played in my life and let him go, gently, lovingly, with deep appreciation for the times we had shared. As his image dissipated, a flood of energy washed over me as if a locked gate had been flung open.

I felt lightheaded as I slipped off the table, like I had been meditating for hours.

"Was that a crystal you put on my chest?" I asked. "It felt heavy and hot."

Annie dropped several tiny amber-colored crystals in the palm of my hand. They weighed almost nothing. "These are what we used," she said with a grin.

"Were they heated?" I asked, confused. I had felt an intense heat shoot straight into my heart area.

"No."

I gazed at the crystals with wide eyes, moving my hand up and down as if trying to feel a weight of some sorts.

"You had a lot of help," Rob said, smiling. "The room was actually filled up, crowded even."

I felt my jaw drop. *They actually saw the angelic beings!* The world of spirit is so delicate, so elusive, like trying to hold on to a dream. My ego mind loved to whisper in my ear that it wasn't real, wasn't tangible, that I was making it all up. Few people who sensed and experienced these things had been part of my life in recent years. I felt *different* from those around me. Like there was nowhere that I belonged. No one I could really talk to. But these people *knew.* They had felt and seen the same thing, confirming my reality, my experiences. They had *validated* those experiences.

"You two are a breath of fresh air," I exclaimed with delight. "You don't know how wonderful it is to have people to talk to, people who understand these things."

They both smiled and hugged me warmly. As I stepped outside, I heard the cry of a raven, as if it were trying to speak to me, as if it were telling me I was doing the right thing, that I was on the right path, that it was all going to be okay.

INNER JOURNEY WITH BREATH AND SOUND

Following Tom's directions, I lay on the mat and began breathing as music rose from two loud speakers placed close to my head. Spiritual music, chants and songs from various cultures, from churches, from temples, from modern spiritual gatherings.

About five minutes into the session, I was suddenly transported to another time, another place. I'm in India, dancing to the beat of drums and cymbals and string instruments. Indian women, no, Indian *goddesses* are dancing around me, swaying, gyrating. We dance ourselves into states of pure ecstasy. *You are one of us,* they whisper.

The scene shifts. Now I am a female monk in a monastery high in the mountains. A male monk enters my cell and proceeds to rape me. I am shaking, afraid. I hear the Indian Goddesses whisper in my mind: "You don't have to accept this reality. You can change it. You have the power."

I have the power to change it. I don't have to accept this! Suddenly the entire scene rewinds, like a movie.

Everything moves backwards. Now I am at the beginning of the scene. The monk enters my cell. I stand up, feeling a rush of power, in charge of my destiny. I raise my hand, sending out all the power I can muster. The man is thrown back against the wall, even though I haven't touched him. He is knocked unconscious. I gather my things and leave the monastery to travel the world.

The scene shifts again. Ghostly images of men begin to line up. Men from other lives. Men with whom I'd experienced sex, but not love. *Cut the cords and set yourself free,* whisper the Indian goddesses. A long knife appears in my hand.

I see ethereal silver cords extending from my midsection, connecting me to these men. I slice through the cords, releasing them one by one. More faces appear--cut, slash, chop. The images emerge faster and faster, dozens, hundreds of them, back through numerous lifetimes. I cut faster and faster. Cut, cut, cut. Like a movie on fast forward, the images transform into an amorphous blur. Slice, sever, slash, cut...

The last ghostly image appears. I slash the cord. He fades away. Energy washes over me. Energy finally freed.

I am back in India, dancing with the goddesses. We move and sway to the music of the drums, dancing ourselves into states of ecstasy. We get lighter and lighter until we lift into the air. I fly above the earth, swirling, swooping, soaring-- feeling light, feeling joyous, feeling free.

I notice Owl by my side. She directs me to follow her. We travel across the earth. It's a dark, moonless night. I see lights coming on, small, flickering lights like candle flames. One here, one there, a third in the distance. They begin to multiply, but there is no particular pattern. A few cluster in one area, while other places remain dark. One lights up in the far distance, then another.

"What are these lights?" I ask Owl, her wings spread wide as she glides by my side.

"They are people waking up."

I look down at the landscape and notice more lights coming on. One, two, a third up on the hill.

"What is causing them to wake up?"

"They are reading your books."

My eyes grow wide with incredulity. "*My* books?"

"Yes."

We soar over the landscape, the lights appearing as if by magic—lonely candles set adrift in a sea of dark.

Meeting Jim Hawk

Jim Hawk was a sixty-ish bear of a man with a white trimmed beard and intense blue eyes. I made a gesture to shake his hand.

"I hug," he said, wrapping me in a firm embrace.

"Claudia said I should meet you," I blurted out, not sure where to begin. "I don't know why."

"If Claudia said we're supposed to meet, than she's probably right." His eyes crinkled mirthfully. We sat in the yard on white plastic lawn chairs.

"In my younger days," he began, leaning back in his chair, "I was in the Special Services, a job that took me to different parts of the world where I worked with indigenous peoples. In my free time, I'd find pieces of wood and diddle with them, carving animals: eagles, ravens, wolves, bears... a skill I'd learned from my grandfather while growing up on a ranch."

I wonder why I'm here? Why was I supposed to meet this man? What am I to learn from this encounter?

Patience, whispered my inner voice. *This meeting is important.*

Feeling a little chilly, I wrapped my thin sweater around me and listened.

"Now, in most tribes, it is the shaman who creates the sacred objects, the ones used for ceremony. My carvings intrigued them. They were curious how I brought the spirit of the animal out of the wood. A relationship would develop and they'd teach me their traditions and beliefs."

An eclectic background. Interesting!

"After I completed my service and moved back to the states, a Hopi shaman named White Bear chose to take me under his wing and teach me the native ways." Jim paused to take a few sips of water. The sun began to set, the weather cooled, and the sky was painted in dramatic rays of orange and pink. I noticed a few bats in the distance, hunting for their evening meal.

Jim continued: "There was this Indian named John. Lived on the reservation. His son was in the hospital, in a coma from a drug overdose. Had been there for some time. The insurance had run out and the hospital wanted to pull the plug. John, terribly worried about his son, wasn't able to come up with the money. Out of options, he turned to the shaman of his tribe."

I sat up straight, all ears.

"The shaman told him to come back in a few days—this is their way—and he'd tell him if he could help his son or not.

"The shaman performed a ceremony and went into trance. White Bear, who had been my teacher, appeared in a vision. 'Send him to Jim Hawk,' he said."

" 'You want me to get help from a white man?' John exclaimed upon his return."

" 'That's the message White Bear gave me,' replied the shaman. So John the Indian began searching for me."

Jim paused as a car drove up. Claudia burst through the gate of Jim's yard, her bubbly personality filling the space.

"Have you seen the feather fans?"

I shook my head. I'd completely forgotten that she had even mentioned the fans.

"She saw the owl," she told Jim.

"I didn't know about the owl," he said, directing us into his workshop which consisted of a central area with several connecting rooms. His artwork included wooden staffs topped with exquisite soapstone carvings – wolf, bear, eagle and owl, wooden pipes, elegant flutes, painted drums and rattles decorated with beads and feathers. A number of elaborate feather fans hung on the wall. I pointed to one that looked particularly pretty. Jim handed it to me.

"How much?" I asked, admiring the beauty of the feathers, the elaborate leather handle, the beads…

"You don't purchase sacred objects," Claudia interjected. "You receive them as gifts. Offering a contribution for the gift is acceptable."

"Oh." I gently lay the fan back on the table. I tossed around possible contribution amounts in my mind as we were given a guided tour of the house, which had been part of an old ranch and had a rich history of its own.

Retiring to an offshoot of the main workshop, Jim sat behind a wide wooden table covered with projects in the making. I admired a thin piece of wood delicately carved into a feather.

Claudia and I settled in white plastic chairs, facing Jim. "Could you tell me the rest of the story of John the Indian?" I asked, prompted by an inner urge, a sense that this story was significant, that I needed to hear the rest.

Jim crossed his legs and leaned back in his chair. "As I was saying, John was directed to seek me out. He showed up at my door one day, insisting he'd been sent by his shaman. 'He sent you to me?' I asked, having a hard time believing this. 'Yes, definitely to you. He had a vision from White Bear. I don't understand it either,' he admitted. I told him to come back in the morning. I'd see what I could do."

I perched on the edge of my chair.

Jim continued: "Now White Bear, my teacher, had taught me about medicine bundles, but he never explained what I was supposed to put in them. Never mentioned anything about bringing a young boy out of a coma. But, I'd promised John I'd help, so I had to do my best. I thought about this long and hard and gathered materials that I believed should go into the bundle, but as soon as I did this, I knew that they weren't quite right. I put them aside, and started over, again, then again. I finally fell asleep at my worktable around three or four in the morning."

I shifted in my chair and folded my arms in front of me. Claudia sat still, listening with attention.

"I woke up at dawn, lifting my head off the worktable, my body stiff, my eyes red. I had done my best, but my best just wasn't good enough. I had to let go and admit that I didn't know what to do. I had to tell John that I couldn't help him."

"Now, my worktable was littered with remnant herbs, plants, feathers, and stones. I grabbed a pouch that I usually use for medicine bags and swept the remnants from the table into the bag, just to put them somewhere, get them off the table. A few feathers were scattered about. I tied these to the bag so they wouldn't fall about the workshop. Just as I hung the bag of remnants on a nail, John's large frame filled the doorway. 'Is this my medicine bundle?' he asked, grabbing it off the wall.

'I guess,' I muttered, not knowing what else to say. He thanked me and left with the bundle."

Jim went quiet for moment, his eyes glassed over as if transported to that time, that place. Claudia and I glanced at each other, then looked back at Jim with anticipation.

His eyes shimmered. "John went to his son, placed the medicine bundle on his chest, and performed ceremony for several days, chanting and praying and hoping. His son showed no change. Finally, he had to accept that it wasn't going to work. Eyes filled with tears, he held his son's hand and said, 'I'm sorry son. I've done everything I could. I'm so sorry.'

John kissed his son and gazed one last time into the boy's young face. He finally rose and dragged himself towards the door, his shoulders sagging, his heart twisted with pain.

Jim paused at this point. The air crackled with tension.

"John stopped at the door, overwhelmed by grief. Suddenly, he heard a voice. 'Don't leave me, Dad,' his son said, 'They'll kill me.'"

A shiver ran up my spine. I folded goose-bumped arms across my chest.

Jim stopped talking, choked up by the memory. Tears escaped the corners of his eyes and rolled down his face, yet he didn't bother to wipe them. Claudia and I sat in stunned silence, the air around us heavy, thick.

"Did the son recover?" I finally asked.

Jim nodded. Pulling himself together, he continued: "Now remember, I had no idea what went into that bundle. They were just bits and pieces of materials leftover on the table. I couldn't duplicate it even if I wanted to. *I* wasn't the one who had decided what went in the bundle." Jim put his hands flat on the table and leaned forward, "It's when I let go of trying to do it, to make it happen with my mind, it's when I got out of the way and admitted that I didn't know how, that Spirit did the work through me. And here is the lesson: *It is when you get out of the way and let Spirit work through you that miracles happen.*"

He sat back in his chair and folded his arms, his eyes deep as the ocean. Those eyes spoke of a knowingness, an understanding, yet at the same time he displayed a humbleness, a humility, as if honoring the presence of something far greater than himself.

"So, are you going to take the fan?" he asked suddenly, leaning forward and piercing me with the intensity of his gaze.

My inner guidance said *no*.

This answer surprised me. *I'm not to take the feather fan?*

No. Not at this time.

I looked up at Jim, not sure what to say. I didn't know if he listened to his spirit guides or followed the still small voice within. I didn't even know if he believed in such things. Playing it safe, I responded: "Maybe I need to learn more about owl medicine before I take the fan."

His demeanor shifted. "Excuse my language," he said, "but *bullshit!* You'll never learn all there is to know about owl medicine."

I cringed, not sure how to respond.

"In your meditation, you received the feather—twice," Claudia said, trying to persuade me that this was the right thing to do.

Do not take the fan at this time, came my inner voice loud and clear. I looked at Claudia, then at Jim and shook my head.

"Well," Jim said, leaning back in his chair, "you can drop by next time you're in town. If it's meant to be yours, it will still be here."

I nodded. "I would like to learn more about owl medicine. Will you teach me?" The words tumbled out of my mouth as if they had a life of their own. *Where did that come from?*

Jim's energy shifted. There was a moment of awkward silence. I thought it best to get up and take my leave when suddenly he shot up and began poking about the workshop, as if animated by the mystery itself. He wandered from place to place, scrounging through boxes, bags, and plastic containers, riffling through piles, searching top shelves and bottom shelves.

The energy in the workshop came to life; it crackled, sparkled. I looked to Claudia for answers. She shook her head and shrugged.

Jim grabbed a small black leather pouch from a hook on the wall and continued to roam around the room, gently, reverently, placing items into the bag: bits of plants and herbs, a tiny crystal, an owl's claw…

I squirmed in my seat, my skin tingling. I had the sensation that something important, no, something *profound* was taking place. I watched Jim as he moved from one end of the workshop to the other.

"What kind of owl did you see?" he asked.

"I, I don't know. It was just an owl. I don't know owls."

He spread a book on the table. "Which one?" he asked.

I flipped through the owl photos. "This one. This is the owl I saw," I pointed to an owl that looked like it had cat ears.

"That's the Great Horned Owl." He pulled several feathers from a large plastic container and wrapped them with twine. I was standing now, arms folded, gaping at the feathers.

Jim fixed his gaze on me, riveting me in place. A presence far beyond Jim the man peered out at me through those cobalt blue eyes. Suddenly, he grabbed my arms and pulled them apart to each side. "Be open to receive," he said. "I was told to tell you that." He placed the feathers and medicine bag in the palms of my hands.

When you receive the feather in physical form, it will be a sign of great learning and wisdom, my guide, Mi-ka-el, had said. I accepted the gifts with a reverence and awe I had never experienced before. Turning to Claudia, I displayed my new treasures with wide eyes.

"You're fast," she said. "You manifested those feathers in just a week."

"A week? I just met you the day before yesterday!"

My head spun as I drove back to the hotel that night, the small bulge of the medicine bag resting near my heart. I wondered if this was how Carlos Castaneda felt when he first met Don Juan Matus. Did he have this feeling of awe, of wonder, the sense that he had just encountered the mystery?

I smiled as I picked up my feather bundle. The feathers were just a symbol, a guide, a means to point me in the right direction.

The *real* feather, the source of learning and wisdom, was Jim Hawk himself.

Spiritual Transformation and Soul Source Union

I stood on the deck of Ranjita's home, up in the canyon, looking over an open grassy area and the rushing waters of Oak Creek. Ranjita, her sandy hair blowing in the breeze, her eyes bright with enthusiasm, was telling me the story of how she came to be in this house and of the spirits of that place. I felt easy with Ranjita, like she was a long-lost friend.

Suddenly, the scenery down near the creek shifted, blurred. Images of an Indian village came into view with women working and children milling about. I was there —I was one of them. I knew this as clearly as I knew my own name. The images dissipated into thin air. I turned to Ranjita, wide-eyed.

"I've lived there," I said, pointing to the grassy area by the creek.

Ranjita stopped what she was saying, her gaze following my pointed finger. "I did, too." Her face beamed. "Maybe we knew each other."

We laughed together and embraced. Her energy felt comfortable, familiar.

I wondered about this as she guided me to her healing room. Maybe part of our spiritual evolution was the understanding of this fact—that through our many lifetimes, we have all lived in different cultures, have had different religions, different skin colors, even different genders. This put in perspective the absurdity of people believing that because of their race, their culture, their country, their religion, or the color of their skin, that they were somehow superior to the other group, while they have probably been and some day will be again the very people they despise.

I lay on the massage table, eyes closed. Ranjita guided me into a meditative state and suggested I look for my inner child. See where I might have left her.

Owl appears, larger than life. I mount her back and we sour into the sky and across the earth all the way to Iran. Owl swoops down and lands in the mountains north of Tehran. A nine-year-old Patti is sitting on a huge boulder by a fresh water spring.

"Did you find her?" Ranjita asked.

"Yes. In Iran. My nine-year-old self is sitting on a boulder, her feet dangling over a fresh water spring. This is a place she loves, a place she feels safe."

"Okay. Now talk to her. Tell her who you are. Tell her you have come to get her. Tell her that you will take her with you, love her, protect her. Tell her, *promise* her that you will never abandon her again."

I slide off Owl's back and approach my child self. She cringes and scoots to the other side of the boulder, a frightened look on her face. I pick up her hand, holding it gently. "I'm sorry I left you here," I say, a pang of guilt twisting my gut. "I didn't know you were here. But I'm here now. I'm going to take care of you. Protect you. I'm going to take you with me. From now on, we'll be together--always." Her face softens, brightens with a wan smile. I move closer and embrace her. She melts into my arms and cries. I let her cry, holding and rocking her, singing to her gently, soothingly. I explain what I'm doing to Ranjita.

"That's good. Now tell her you are going to take her with you and bring her back."

"Do you want to come with me?" I ask, squatting low to look into her face. She nods. I gather her into my arms and mount Owl, holding my younger self in front of me. She squeals with delight when Owl spreads her wings and takes flight. We return to Sedona.

"We're back," I tell Ranjita.

"Okay, now embrace your inner child and take her into your heart."

I hold my child and whisper in her ear. Slowly, she disappears and melts into my heart.

Ranjita places my hands across my heart. "Now keep her there, safe and sound."

I sense my inner child. She is no longer lost, no longer alone, but now and forever a part of me, comfortable and safe and loved.

AND THE MISSION IS...

I returned to Hawai`i, feeling refreshed, renewed, and clearer about my purpose than ever before. While I sensed the changes would take a while to settle in and become a part of me, I felt, I sensed, I *knew* that a stuckness had been released from my physical body, my energy field, and my mind. I had a sensation of flow, of movement, of changes to come.

I had gained a general "map" of my purpose. I am on a quest for truth, wherever it takes me, pushing the limits of human understanding. My purpose involves opening my heart to love and compassion and sharing that with the world. My way is the way of the mystic, the one who sees the bigger picture, the one who serves the greater good. I can manifest this in the world by reaching wholeness and balance within myself, then sharing how I did it by writing about it, by talking about it to individuals and groups. My job is to help people wake up to who they really are.

My life did not change overnight, but change it did, over the following months and years. Instead of paying attention to my inner critique, I decided to improve my writing skills by taking classes, workshops, seminars, and attending writing conferences. I still struggled, unsure of which life events to write about, what words to use, how to convey these intense emotional experiences, wondering if any of this would ring true, trying desperately to find the time to write and revise. I sensed that my craft was improving, but everything still seemed to be moving at a snail's pace.

Mark's appraisal business was doing well and he also began to build and sell spec homes. Over time, our financial picture improved and Mark suggested that I let go of my university job and do what I wanted to do. Although my university salary wasn't significant, I was reluctant. I was used to having my regular paychecks. They gave me a sense of independence. A sense of self worth. I also identified myself as a university faculty and a program director. If I let go of that, what would I be? Mark's position was that I already had the years necessary to get my pension; that his salary was pushing me into a higher tax bracket; that I needed the time to do what I wanted to do.

I took regular trips to Sedona and met again with Claudia and Debra and Tom and Ranjita and learned from the wisdom of Jim Hawk. Mark and I loved to visit the many art galleries and hike through the magnificent red rocks. When a new subdivision opened up, we purchased land for our retirement. Slowly, my need to rush or manipulate things and events subsided as I realized all is going forward as it should be.

SPRING 2006, HAWAI'I

It was just after dark. The moon rose above the o'hia trees and spilled into the room while the koqui frogs sang their never-ending mating song. The tapered candle flame illumined the objects on my altar: an assortment of crystals in clusters, pyramids, and globes; the Egyptian Goddess Isis, healer of body, mind, and spirit, holding the ankh, symbol of eternal life; Yemaya, African Goddess of the sea who dissolves one's troubles in the waters of her embrace; Sarasvati, Hindu Goddess of creative arts and wisdom; Kwan-Yin, Chinese Goddess of merciful compassion, Innanna, Sumerian Goddess who helps bond spirit and body into ecstatic union; Ganesh, the elephant-headed God of India, mover of obstacles, opener of new paths; a small figure of owl, my totem animal, my guide; a brass Tibetan bowl with an otherworldly chime; a string of crystal beads from Nepal; various feathers, some found, some gifted; Teiwaz, rune of the spiritual warrior. Sacred objects, symbols, archetypes from different cultures of the world, from people on their sacred path to comprehend the mystery, to connect with the divine.

Our origins are clear—all of us God-sparks, pieces of the divine. Our destination is certain—we all, ultimately, return to oneness, to the mind of God. In the end, the experiences we have, the lives we touch, the wisdom we gain, the *journey itself* is what matters.

The room is heady with the scent of incense and sage. The candle flame flickers. The mystery calls to me. I smile. I now know how to answer the call. Calming body and mind, I slip into a meditative state.

What is the next step on my path?
Write.
That's it?
That's it for the moment. Write your story and share it with others. This is all you need do right now.
And Sedona?
You will be there in the perfect time.

* * * * *

Don Juan Matus had directed Carlos Castaneda to collect an album of memorable events that had changed him profoundly. This art of *recapitulation*, which resulted in Carlo's final book, *The Active Side of Infinity*, would free one's energy, energy that had been stuck in these past events. After reading Carlos's final book, I realized that my inner spirit had given me a similar directive. *God Outside the Box* is *my* recapitulation.

And so, in the Fall of 2006, I took the leap, left the University of Hawaii, and poured my soul into the writing of this book. I wrote with a passion, an energy, and an enthusiasm that I had never experienced before. I was on fire, erupting like Pele's volcano, spewing out my stories page after page, chapter after chapter. I was a woman with a mission, a purpose, a calling to something greater than myself. I did not need priest or rabbi or mullah or guru or any of the holy scriptures of the world to tell me why I'm here and what I am to do. I *knew*. I knew in my soul. I knew in my bones. I knew in my very DNA. What I knew could be synthesized simply, easy to comprehend:

My purpose is to spread seeds of awakening. Awakening of the heart.

Mission accepted.

Bibliography

"101 Great Quotes." http://newperspectives.com/free/quotes.html (Oct. 15, 2001).

The Academy for Future Science. *"The Holy Spirit: The Feminine Aspect of the Godhead."* 2003. http://www.pistissophia.org/The_Holy_Spirit/the_holy_spirit html (Nov. 5, 2004).

BBC – Religion and Ethics. *"Beliefs of Hinduism."* http://www.bbc.co.uk/relgions/Hinduism/beliefs/index.shtml (May 19, 2004).

The Celtic Connection. *"The Concept of Deity."* http://wicca.com/celtic/wicca/concepts.htm (Nov. 4, 2004).

The Christian Science Monitor. *"Islam: Beliefs and Practices."* http://www.csmonitor.com/2001/1115/p18sl-lire.html (May 18, 2004).

"Chronology of People's Park – The Old Days." Based in part on Alan Copeland's People's Park. http://users.rcn.com/hi-there/tmlin2.html (Nov. 9, 2004).

Griscom, Chris. Ecstasy is a New Frequency. New York: Simon & Schuster, 1988.

Huna.com. *"Excerpt from the Lost Secrets of Ancient Hawaiian Huna, Volume 1, Chapter1."* http://www.huna.com/hunach1.html (Sept. 17, 2003).

Indian Sun. *"The Huichol Culture."* 1999. http://www.indiansun.net/huichol.htm (April 12, 2004).

MSN Encarta. *"Zoroastrianism."* http://encarta.msn.com/encyclopedia_761558789/zoroastrianism.html (May 18, 2004).

National Gandhi Museum. *"Gandhi – Inner Voice and Vows."* (Harijan, 8.7.1933) http://meadev.nic.in/Gandhi/innervoice.htm (Sept. 21, 2004).

Pardes Spiritual Education. *"The Inner Voice According to Rav Kook."* http://www2.pardes.org.il/spiritualeducation/principles/inner_voice.php (Sept. 22, 2004).

Religious Tolerance.org. *"Hinduism: A General Introduction."* http://www.religioustolerance.org/hinuism2.htm (May 19, 2004).

Religious Tolerance.org. *"Zoroastriansim: Founded by Zarathushtra."* http://www.religioustolerance.org/zoroastr.htm (May 18, 2004).

Scott-Mana, Robin Osunnike. *"Ase Whole Life Healing System."* http://www.theafrican.com/Healer/Ossunike/InstofTransHeal.html (April 12, 2004).

Sufism-Beliefnet.com. *"Great Hafiz Quote."* http://www.beliefnet.com/boards/message_list.asp?discussionID-397981 (1/25/08).

The Universal Worship of Hazrat Inayat Khan. *"Unity and Uniformity."*
http://www.sufimovement.org/uniworship.htm (Sept. 21, 04)

The Watchman Expositor. *"Unity School of Christianity (Unity)."* http://www.watchman.org/cults/untychart.html (Sept. 21, 2004)

"Who Owns the Park." http://users.rcn.com/hi-there/gerbwin.html (Nov. 9, 2004)

The Witches Way. *"Pagan Beliefs."* http://www.witchesway.net/links/paganism/beliefs.html
(Nov. 4, 2004).

Patricia Panahi holds a BA in English and an MA in Linguistics from San Diego State University. She spent twenty years teaching English to international students in Iran, California, and Hawaii. She also directed ESL programs for Hawaii Community College and the University of Hawaii at Hilo.

In the mid 1980's, she owned and operated The Light Spot, a metaphysical bookstore and coffeehouse in San Diego. She also managed the Inner Visions Center which offered classes and workshops on personal transformation.

Patricia currently devotes her time to writing and her spitirual path. She lives on the Big Island of Hawaii with her husband and one mischievous feline.

Printed in the United States
110012LV00001B/75/P